⤛ OLD ⤜
CHARLESTON
ORIGINALS
FROM CELEBRITIES TO SCOUNDRELS

MARGARET MIDDLETON RIVERS EASTMAN

THE
History
PRESS

Published by The History Press
Charleston, SC 29403
www.historypress.net

Cover images: Front images (Jenkins Orphanage and the South Carolina Hall on Meeting Street) are courtesy of the Charleston Museum, Charleston, South Carolina. On back, the image of Aunt Phoebe is from the Library of Congress, and the Marshlands image is courtesy of the *Charleston Mercury*, Charleston, South Carolina.

First published 2011

ISBN 978.1.60949.252.6

Library of Congress Cataloging-in-Publication Data

Eastman, Margaret Middleton Rivers.
Old Charleston originals : from celebrities to scoundrels / Margaret Middleton Rivers
Eastman.
p. cm.
Includes bibliographical references.
ISBN 978-1-60949-252-6
1. Charleston (S.C.)--Biography. 2. Charleston (S.C.)--History. I. Title.
F279.C453A243 2011
975.7'915--dc23
2011018254

In loving memory of my parents
Marwee and Mendel Rivers

CONTENTS

Drawing by Milton Caniff.

Introduction

L. MENDEL RIVERS

R ivers served as Charleston's Democratic Congressman for the First District between 1940 and 1970. Born in the tiny rural hamlet of Gumville, in Berkeley County, Rivers—the son of a [prominent[1]] rural farmer—became one of the nation's leading political figures in the global power-struggle with the Soviet Union.

Gradually ascending to the powerful chairmanship of the House Armed Services Committee, the monumentally self-confident Rivers exercised his clout on Capitol Hill by luring thousands of military jobs to the Lowcountry in the decades following World War II. In the 1950s, he successfully lobbied for the establishment of the Charleston Air Force Base. Private defense contractors located plants in Charleston as well, redefining the region as an outpost of the military-industrial complex.

A 1969 survey by the Charleston Chamber of Commerce found that payrolls for military bases pumped $317 million into the local economy, accounting for 55 percent of the region's total payroll at that time. This excessive dependence on military employment led to a long-standing joke that Charleston actually boasted "three rivers," the Ashley, the Cooper and Mendel Rivers. Today his surname is emblazoned on both Rivers Avenue and the Rivers Annex Post Office.

A bold and often controversial figure, Rivers regularly lambasted '60s Secretary of Defense Robert McNamara over the nation's policies during the unpopular Vietnam War. Notorious wag and nationally syndicated newspaper columnist Drew Pearson frequently attacked Rivers for what was called his pork-barrel political style.

INTRODUCTION

In October 1970, the Reverend Billy Graham dedicated the L. Mendel Rivers Library at the Baptist College, now Charleston Southern University. Nearly two months later, Rivers died of heart failure. Twenty-one years after Rivers' death, the Iron Curtain collapsed.

Ultimately, Rivers' beloved Charleston Navy Base became a casualty of the Pentagon's post–Cold War downsizing. Despite the military's waning presence in Charleston, Mendel Rivers kept the Lowcountry afloat during the post–World War II era, a transition which led today's growing, white-hot economy.

–Walter Edgar, Harlan Greene, Cynthia Jenkins,
Robert Rosen and Gene Waddell[2]

ACKNOWLEDGEMENTS

C harles Witte Waring III, editor of the *Charleston Mercury*, for permitting adaptation of articles that first appeared in the *Mercury* and for giving me the opportunity to get to know Charleston better.

Marie Ferrara, Anne Bennett, Claire Fund, Angela Flenner, Deborah Larsen, Sam Stewart and John White of the College of Charleston Special Collections Library, who have provided years of assistance and friendship.

Carl Borick, assistant director, Jennifer Scheetz, archivist, and Jan Hiester, registrar, of the Charleston Museum for invaluable support throughout the years.

Margaret (Marwee) Middleton Rivers, who left behind a treasury of writings, some of which are included in this volume.

Mendel Rivers Jr., for the story about Colonel Joseph Evans Jenkins at the Secession Convention.

Dorothy Middleton Anderson, who introduced me to A. Toomer Porter and *Hampton and His Red Shirts*.

Frank Barnwell, Joseph Cockrell and Fleetwood Hassell, for research on the Charleston Bible Society.

Quentin Baxter and Jack McCrae, for background information on Lowcountry music and Charleston jazz.

Amelia P. Cathcart, Ruth Knopf and Jane Waring, for introducing me to the world of heritage roses.

Charles (Charlie) Henry Drayton III and Anne Drayton Nelson, for insights about the Drayton family.

Jim and Ann Edwards, who shared their history-making life experiences.

Helen Pringle Gibbs, who patiently helped edit and provided information about the Ball family.

To Langhorne Moultrie Howard, for sharing her mother's efforts to save Marshlands and a peek at her father's love of aviation and love for our country.

Harriott Pinckney Means Johnson, for her research about the railroad contributions of the Parsons family.

Dr. George W. McDaniel, Kristine Morris and Natalie Baker, for invaluable assistance with Drayton Hall's history.

Fred MaDan, for background on 93 Rutledge Avenue.

Bert and Helen Pruitt, for providing information on 54 Meeting Street and its builder, Timothy Ford.

Jane Thornhill Schachte, Jane Lucas Thornhill and Elizabeth Jenkins Young and her family, for sharing their rich heritage.

Ted Stern, for sharing his exceptional life story.

Robert Stockton, *News and Courier*'s "Do You Know Your Charleston" columnist and professor of architecture and history at the College of Charleston, for keeping me on track.

Seabrook Wilkerson, for helpful editing and support.

To the wonderful gang at The History Press who helped with this book: Jessica Berzon, Katie Parry, Dan Watson, Ryan Finn, Julie Foster, Natasha Momberger, Jamie Barreto, Adam Ferrell and Brittain Phillips.

To those who helped along the way: Wayne Braverman, Colby Broadwater, Nick Butler, Marion and Wayland Cato, Richard Donohoe, Edward Good, Christopher Liberatos, Martha Meeker, Candice Solyan, Evan Thompson, Lish Thompson, Rutledge Young Jr. and Rutledge Young III.

Margaret (Peg) Middleton Rivers Eastman
June 15, 2011

THE GOOSE CREEK MEN

COLONIAL BARBADOS

Between 1640 and 1670, the tiny island of Barbados produced a culture that, with only slight alteration, would be replicated throughout the English Caribbean islands and along the South Carolina coast.

English sailors had first landed on Barbados in 1625. Finding it uninhabited, they took possession in the name of James I; settlers arrived soon afterward. At that time, events in the Caribbean did not affect the political affairs of European nations. As a result, the island became a lawless frontier on the edge of civilization where might was right and social restraints gave way to the pursuit of wealth and its pleasures. Barbados was plagued by greed on land and by pirates at sea.

In the early days, the Barbadian colonists struggled to survive by exporting tobacco and cotton. Most of the inhabitants were indentured white males, some of whom had been kidnapped by unscrupulous labor suppliers. The practice was so widespread that the term "Barbadoed" had the same meaning then that "Shanghaied" acquired two hundred years later.

With the introduction of sugar cane from Brazil in the 1640s, however, the entire culture of the colony changed. The seemingly insatiable worldwide demand for sugar, and its byproducts rum and molasses, made growing sugar cane enormously profitable. Barbados soon became the richest colony in English America.

The allure of attainable wealth captured the attention of English adventurers. They flocked to the tiny island, causing the price of land to skyrocket. With only 100,000 acres of arable land, it was not long before large plantation estates began to displace the modest holdings of early settlers. By 1670, the wealthiest plantations averaged about 200 acres, although nearly half of the landowners owned less than 10 acres. As fortunes were made, some Barbadians returned to England, leaving their lands to be managed by hirelings.

But for even the most prosperous, there was a dark side to this island paradise. It was cheaper for planters to purchase African slaves for life than it was to contract with indentured white males who worked for a few years. Additionally, white servants from the British Isles required more expensive food, clothing and shelter. Economics—not race—caused the planters to switch to an African labor force. Within in a very short period, enslaved Africans were being imported by the thousands and quickly outnumbered the white settlers. Slave uprisings were the inevitable result and effected the enactment of repressive slave codes as early as 1661.

During the early stages of civil war in England, Barbados became an asylum for both Royalists (Cavaliers) and Parliamentarians (Roundheads).

The island of Barbados divided into its parishes, by Herman Moll (1654–1732).

Although Royalists were in the majority, they lived amicably together until King Charles I was beheaded in 1649. After his execution, a victorious Oliver Cromwell and the Parliamentarians sought to punish the Royalists in the sugar islands for their allegiance to the Crown. They enacted restrictive trade laws that prohibited colonial trade with foreign nations without a license from the Council of State.

Once royal authority was reestablished in 1660, Barbadians looked for some relief from Charles II. Instead, the capricious king rewarded only thirteen Royalists with empty titles for their loyalty and sufferings. One of them was John Colleton, who had fought for the Royalists. Once parliamentary forces had succeeded in England, he had immigrated to Barbados. When Charles II ascended the throne, he returned to London to seek reward for his support. Through the intervention of his old friend John Berkeley, Baron Berkeley of Stratton, he was knighted and appointed to the Council on Foreign Plantations. There he came in contact with some of the most powerful lords of the realm: Sir William Berkeley, Sir Anthony Ashley Cooper (later Earl of Shaftesbury), Sir George Carteret and Edward Hyde, Earl of Clarendon. In addition, Colleton's cousin was George Monck, Duke of Albemarle. With his colonial experience, Colleton was able to interest his associates in developing North America south of Virginia.

In 1663, eight of Charles's powerful supporters requested and received a charter for the Colony of Carolina. The king was extremely generous with his grant; it included all of the land south of Virginia and extended west to the Pacific Ocean. In addition, he granted taxing and legislative powers usually enjoyed by a ruling monarch. With their paper empire, the Lords Proprietor had an opportunity to establish a model colony in the new world, and the opportunities for making money seemed infinite.[3]

The Lords Proprietor hoped to populate their holdings with experienced settlers from other established colonies. As land was plentiful, generous inducements were made to attract colonists from the already overcrowded English Caribbean islands.

The cash-strapped king and his ministers ignored many other Royalists in Barbados. To raise revenue, they levied an irrevocable and permanent tax to be applied to the satisfaction of land claims then in question, with the remainder to be placed at the disposal of the Crown. Many loyal subjects found themselves being taxed out of their estates. A destructive locust plague, a series of major hurricanes and a disastrous fire in Bridgetown also contributed to their woes. It was no wonder that beleaguered Barbadian planters determined to join in exploration and settlement of the Carolina coast.[4]

PROPRIETARY GOVERNMENT

The Lords Proprietor's idea of a model state was, of course, aristocratic. They had no idea of setting up a government ruled by a "too numerous democracy." Their vivid recollections of Cromwell and his cohorts prevented any such foolishness. Anthony Ashley Cooper, the Earl of Shaftesbury, commissioned John Locke to write a constitution for governing the new colony. In it the Proprietors delegated authority to their representatives and retained a veto power over their acts. The ruling colonial Grand Council consisted of a governor and proprietary representatives, an upper house of ten colonials selected by the leading landowners and a Commons House of Assembly composed of twenty members selected by landed "freedmen." Although power of the Commons House was originally limited to discussion of proposals from the other two parts of the Grand Council, by 1682 all three groups had to approve any act, and the Commons House had gained the power for legislative initiative. The constitution set up the division of the land, protected slavery and granted religious freedoms to non-Catholic settlers.[5]

The earliest Carolina arrivals were given an opportunity to become titled landholders. All they needed was enough money to purchase the land. Depending on one's pocketbook, one might become a baron, cassique or landgrave. A thriving aristocracy was soon established, for land could be grabbed up for one penny per acre.

Many of the earliest settlers were from Barbados, and they were quickly joined by men from the other English Caribbean Islands.[6] Those first settlers pushed their trading posts as far as the Mississippi River one hundred years before Daniel Boone explored Kentucky. Indian trading (furs, skins and Indian slaves) was so lucrative that the beloved Indian agent and explorer Henry Woodward earned a salary equal to that of the proprietary governor.

A great number of Barbadian planters settled in the Goose Creek area; they were politically united by their common desire to preserve the enormous profits made through the illegal Indian slave trade and trafficking with pirates, who brought their ill-gotten goods to Charles Towne and sold them at a fraction of the going rate. Led primarily by Sir John Yeamans, Maurice Mathews, Robert Daniell, James Moore, James Moore Jr. and Arthur Middleton, they gained control of the Commons House of Assembly during the early years of the colony, and the Proprietors soon learned to be wary of the "Goose Creek men."[7]

The Remarkable Men from Goose Creek

The ambitious Sir John Yeamans (1611–1674) was the son of a Bristol alderman who had been beheaded during the English civil war.

In 1650, after Charles I was beheaded, Yeamans immigrated to Barbados, where he already owned land. He became a judge and a member of council. After Cromwell's rule ended, he was rewarded with a title for his loyalty to the Crown.

The Proprietors appointed him governor of the Cape Fear settlement in 1665, but shortly after the colony was founded, Yeamans deserted the colonists to attend to his affairs in Barbados. (After much tribulation, the colony was abandoned in 1667.)

Once home, Yeamans found that recent hurricanes had severely damaged his plantations; his personal life was also a disaster. He had gone into a land partnership with Colonel Benjamin Berringer. When Berringer found out that Yeamans had been conducting an ill-concealed affair with his wife, he challenged him to a duel. The aggrieved husband was killed, and ten weeks later, Yeamans married pregnant Margaret Berringer and moved in with his new bride. When the land grab was contested, the Barbados court rather quickly ruled that the property could not be merged with Yeamans's holdings and returned it to Berringer's children.

Meanwhile, back in England, Anthony Ashley Cooper had convinced the parsimonious Lords Proprietor to attempt another Carolina settlement. In 1669, they financed outfitting three ships (*Carolina*, *Port Royal* and *Albemarle*), loaded them with potential colonists and directed them to settle in Port Royal. The ships stopped in Ireland to recruit servants and proceeded on to Barbados in the hope of attracting more settlers. With his plantations all but destroyed, it was fortuitous that Sir John Yeamans had been named a landgrave in the Fundamental Constitutions. Instructed to name a governor, Yeamans named himself and joined the expedition.

While still in Barbados, a gale wrecked the *Albemarle* on the rocky coast; Yeamans hired the *Three Brothers* as a replacement. The three ships set sail during hurricane season and were scattered by storms near the island of Nevis. The *Port Royal* wrecked near Abaco in the Bahamas. The *Carolina* and the *Three Brothers* eventually landed in Bermuda, where some of the *Port Royal* survivors managed to rejoin them.

In January 1670, while still in Bermuda, Yeamans decided to return to Barbados, this time giving the excuse that he needed to be part of the commission negotiating with the French about evicting English settlers from

St. Christopher's Island in 1666. Yeamans persuaded the colonists to let the eighty-year-old former Bermuda governor, William Sayle, take his place, in the hope that Sayle would attract some of his countrymen to the expedition. Sayle's name was duly put on the blank commission that Yeamans had received from the Proprietors. The other colonists considered Sayle an aged, Puritanical bigot.[8] Others on the commission were Joseph West, deputy for the Duke of Albemarle; Dr. William Scrivener for Lord Berkeley; Stephen Bull for Lord Ashley; William Bowman for Lord Craven; and Florence O'Sullivan.[9]

In April 1670, the English settlers landed at Albemarle Point on the west bank of the Ashley River and founded Charles Towne, naming it in honor of Charles II.

Among passengers on the *Carolina* was Affra Harleston, a gentlewoman of reduced circumstances, who immigrated to the new colony as a single woman, paying for her passage by contracting for two years of indentured service. She afterward married John Coming, first mate of the *Carolina* and later captain of the *Blessing.* For his services as a sea captain, Coming received land grants on the Cooper River. Captain Coming and Lieutenant Henry Hughes also took out grants for land at the confluence of the Ashley and Cooper Rivers at Oyster Point.

As landgrave, Yeamans arrived at the new Carolina colony in 1671 fully expecting to become governor. However, in his absence, Governor Sayle had died, and Joseph West had been appointed interim governor until the Lords Proprietor could appoint a replacement. Yeamans became the third governor over the objections of members of the Grand Council, who decried his earlier desertion of both Carolina settlements.

The colonists soon discovered that Albemarle Point was inconvenient and unhealthy, and Governor Yeamans issued an order for the "laying out of a town" at Oyster Point. Coming, his wife, Affra, and Hughes appeared before the Grand Council and offered to give up half of their lands on Oyster Point for the town site.[10]

Governor Yeamans had brought two hundred African slaves with him, and they set about clearing his lands; the lumber was exported to Barbados. The governor soon acquired the reputation of being out only for himself. He angered Shaftesbury when he profited by selling provisions to Barbados when they were desperately needed in Carolina. Called a "sordid calculator" bent solely on acquiring a fortune, he was finally removed from office and died before news of his replacement by Joseph West arrived in Charles Towne.[11] Biographers have since described Yeamans as everything from a swashbuckling cavalier to a land pirate.

The Goose Creek Men

Maurice Mathews was the nephew of two of the Earl of Shaftesbury's friends; at one point, he was also Shaftesbury's deputy. Part of the original settlement, he was a passenger on the *Three Brothers*. En route to Carolina, the sloop had been blown off course and was driven on to the island of St. Catherine. Captain John Rivers (Lord Ashley's deputy) and several passengers went ashore for water; they were captured by the local Indians at

A Plan of the Town & Harbor of Charles Town from A Compleat Description of the Province of Carolina in 3 Parts; 1st the improved part from the surveys of Maurice Matthews & Mr. John Love; 2ly, the west part of Capt. Tho. Nairn; 3ly, a chart of the coast from Virginia to Cape Florida by Edward Crisp, circa 1710. Courtesy College of Charleston Special Collections Library, Waddell Collection, Charleston, South Carolina.

the instigation of a Spanish friar living there. The sloop managed to escape, but the unfortunate captives did not and were transported to St. Augustine, where they all died while in prison. [12]

Mathews was a member of the Grand Council and eventually became the colony's surveyor general. As the Fundamental Constitutions required that the whole province be surveyed, this was a position of great importance. Mathews surveyed as far south as Florida. His work has been preserved on the Edward Crisp map of 1710.

Mathews was also commissioner to the Indians. The Indian trade produced the primary exports of the early colony: animal skins, furs and Indian slaves. His political opponents disliked his practices and called him "Metchivell Hobs and Lucifer in a Huge lump of Viperish mortality [with] a soul [as] big as a musketo."[13] In 1685, Mathews was removed from office for illegal Indian slave trafficking.[14]

The political events in England greatly influenced the Carolina colony. Their primary guiding force, Anthony Ashley Cooper, fell from grace in 1673 and was imprisoned in the Tower of London on more than one occasion. In 1681, he was exiled to Amsterdam, where he died in 1683. Sir William Craven, the first Earl of Craven, replaced Shaftesbury as the proprietary leader in 1681. James II succeeded his brother to the throne in 1685. His autocratic policies and Roman Catholicism caused him to be deposed in the "Glorious Revolution of 1688."

Parliament and the English populace in general were sick of Roman Catholic monarchs and the upheavals they had caused. Instead of choosing James II's son, James Francis Edward, his Protestant sister, Mary, and her husband, William of Orange, were invited to co-reign.

It was during the political turmoil in England that Craven sought to diminish the Goose Creek men's power in the Carolinas. He theorized that he could defeat their purposes by increasing the non-Anglican majority who already outnumbered the Church of England settlers from the islands. He removed the Goose Creek men from office and denied them access to the profitable Indian trade. In 1686, Craven appointed James Colleton, brother of Sir John Colleton, governor with the rank of landgrave and endowed him with forty-eight thousand acres of land. Colleton was tasked with investigating the relations between the colony's leaders and the pirates who were wreaking havoc in the Caribbean.

Shortly after Governor Colleton's arrival, the Spanish raided some coastal plantations and the Scottish settlement at Stewart Town. The colonists wanted revenge, and Colleton declared martial law to stop an ill-advised retaliatory expedition to Spanish Florida. Martial law kept the Goose Creek men at bay for a time.

But Colleton was no match for his wily antagonists, and he soon found himself in serious trouble. They gained his confidence, proposed that he deserved to increase his salary and suggested instituting an excise tax on imported liquors. Colleton took the bait, and the Goose Creek men promptly voted against the act and accused the governor of trying to enslave and ruin the people. The ensuing hullabaloo forced Colleton to dissolve the 1689 Parliament and rendered the government impotent. Luckily for Colleton, England was at war with France, and Colleton placed the colony under martial law once again.

Until threats posed by the French disappeared, the Goose Creek men were silenced. Then Seth Southall arrived from North Carolina. Southall had purchased the Earl of Clarendon's interest in the Proprietorship after his death, and he had been appointed governor of both Albemarle and Charles Town. He had governed North Carolina until 1689, when he was deposed and expelled for a year because of his corruption. Instead of answering those charges in England, he went to Charles Town. The Goose Creek men used his arrival as a pretext to remove Colleton in 1690. (Colleton was barred from holding office and banished. He died in Barbados in 1707.)

Southall may have learned something from his experiences in Albemarle, but his greedy ways caused him to be ousted once again in 1691.[15] Both Robert Daniell and James Moore incurred the Proprietors' wrath by supporting Southall.

Robert Daniell (1646–1718) had emigrated from Barbados and earned a good name for himself repelling the Spanish when they invaded the colony in 1686. After Southall's expulsion, Daniell returned to England, where he somehow managed to get back into the Proprietors' good graces. While there, he helped with the final version of the Fundamental Constitutions and received a patent as landgrave. Daniell returned to the colony in 1697 and soon became one of the leaders of the Goose Creek men.

Because of his highhanded methods while commanding the continental militia in 1702, Daniell was deemed "a person of notorious ill fame & Conversation." The House refused to let him command the expedition against St. Augustine, so Daniell had to content himself by serving as second in command under James Moore. As part of the amphibious assault, he sailed on to Jamaica for supplies and was almost captured by the Spaniards upon his return to Florida.

Daniell was commended for his bravery when he returned to Charles Town, but having had enough of the military, he turned down other opportunities for service.

Sir Nathaniel Johnson appointed Daniell deputy governor for North Carolina in 1704. After Daniell became involved in a controversy with Quaker settlers, he was removed from that office. An Anglican clergyman in North Carolina characterized him as "monster Wickedness," someone who could be bought and sold. Daniell returned to South Carolina.

In 1715, during the Yemassee War, Daniell led a force that pushed the Indians into Florida. When Governor Craven left the province in 1716, he appointed Daniell deputy governor, but he was replaced because of his opposition to the proprietary faction in the legislature. As landgrave, Daniell was entitled to 48,000 acres of land. He received 31,247 acres, most of which he sold. At the time of his death, he still owned 1,519 acres, 700 of which were on an island in the Wando River that continues to bear his name (though now rendered as "Daniel").[16]

Daniell's confederate, James Moore, immigrated to Carolina from Barbados in 1675, bringing thirty-seven slaves with him. Most historians believe that Moore's father was Rory O'Moore, leader of the Irish Rebellion in 1641. He managed William Walley's Goose Creek plantation for eight years before he obtained a land grant for 2,400 acres near Goose Creek where he established two plantations of his own, Boochawee Hall and Wassamassaw.

In addition to being a merchant who was part owner of two vessels, Moore was in the fur trade, trafficked with pirates and engaged in the illegal Indian trade. He traveled six hundred miles into the interior searching for additional trade opportunities. In 1683, the Proprietors dismissed him as a proprietary deputy because he enslaved Indians. Moore held numerous elective and appointed offices and, by 1692, was the acknowledged leader of the Goose Creek men. It did not hurt that he married Margaret Berringer, stepdaughter of Governor Yeamans.

As a result of his connections, Moore was able to get back in the good graces of the Proprietors after the Southall affair and returned to the Council. When Governor Blake died in 1700, Moore was elected to fill the vacancy. Two years later, during the War of Spanish Succession (Queen Anne's War), Moore commanded the expedition to capture St. Augustine, Florida. The Carolinians besieged the Castillo de San Marcos. When Spanish reinforcements arrived, the Carolinians burned the town and went back home.

Although the Florida expedition was unsuccessful in eliminating the Spanish threat, Moore regained his reputation as a military commander when he led an expedition that exterminated their allies, the Apalachee Indians. He was replaced as governor by Sir Nathaniel Johnson in 1703. Moore was attorney general on the Council and held other high offices before he died of distemper in 1707.[17]

Governor Moore was the great-grandfather of the controversial Revolutionary War general Robert Howe, whose paternal ancestor was Captain Job Howe of Howe Hall. Howe owned several plantations in St. James Goose Creek Parish. He held the officers of surveyor and surveyor general and served three consecutive terms as Speaker of Commons Assembly House (1700 to 1705). In 1700, Speaker Howe supported an act for a provincial library and was named a commissioner and a trustee. Howe died in 1706 during the yellow fever epidemic.[18]

As Speaker, Howe apparently had great oratorical talents. This ability got him into trouble during a legislative session and precipitated the earliest recorded duel in the Carolinas. One evening, while the gentlemen were out entertaining themselves, Howe vowed to thrash John Stewart in front of Governor Johnson.

Stewart was a strong proprietary supporter, who had been placed in charge of Colleton's Wadboo Barony at the head of the Cooper River. He had received several grants of land in appreciation for his experiments in silk production and the growth of other commodities.[19] He had a high opinion of himself and took up the challenge.

The duel had all of the elements of a seventeenth-century farce. The antagonists and their seconds met in the woods in the early morning hours. Both men drew their swords, faced each other and waited. Neither moved. They stood still for a full six minutes. Stewart claimed afterward that Howe, being the aggressor, should have struck first. During the interminable standoff, two constables sent by the governor arrived to stop the bloodshed. Stewart's second grabbed his arm, whereupon Howe struck Stewart with a hickory stick and ran off.

Stewart later wrote to William Dunlop that he had jerked his arm free, drawn his "scymetar" and chased his assailant, swinging his sword within an inch of Howe's retreating neck. Stewart claimed that he sent Howe word that he "was a better Trimmer of Politicks than a swordsman and bid him tell him that...he was a cowardly roage and a great lyar." Although the bold Stewart claimed that Howe had become the mockery of the town, he wrote in the same letter that he was forced to sleep in his bed with both a naked sword and a charged gun as protection from the local Goose Creek citizenry."[20]

By contrast, Robert Gibbes was considered a more moderate member of the Goose Creek faction. Born in 1644 in England, he immigrated to Barbados and is thought to have assisted in some of the planning of the Carolina colony after its charter was granted. He arrived in April 1692 on the *Loyal Jamaica*, "a ship commonly called the Privateer Vessel" because all the passengers were placed under bond. Gibbes was made a member of the General Assembly from Colleton County the year of his arrival and received substantial land due to his bringing numerous slaves.[21] By 1700, he was resident of a plantation between the Cooper and Ashley Rivers (later known as Lowndes Grove). His early connections with the Proprietors helped him to rise quickly in colonial politics, and in 1708, the Proprietors appointed him chief justice of South Carolina.

Gibbes's career was not without controversy. When Governor Tynte died in 1710, only three duly appointed deputies were in the province: Thomas Broughton, Fortesque Turbeville and Robert Gibbes. According to the Fundamental Constitutions, one was to assume the governorship until the Proprietors selected a successor.

One morning, the deputies met to vote for a governor and then recessed until the afternoon. When they reconvened, Gibbes was proclaimed governor. It was later discovered that Broughton had received a two-to-one vote in the morning, and Gibbes was thought to have bribed Turbeville to change his vote during the recess. Turbeville died suddenly and people claimed that he had been poisoned.

Incensed, Broughton collected armed supporters at his plantation and marched to Charles Town. When Gibbes heard of their approach, he ordered a general alarm and had the drawbridge hauled up. Broughton later gained entrance to the town, but to preserve peace, he permitted Gibbes to remain acting governor until the Proprietors selected a replacement.

The Tuscarora War began in North Carolina while Gibbes was in office, and he dispatched Colonel James Moore and Colonel John Barnwell to Albemarle. Before he left office, he cited his accomplishments as the encouragement of white immigration to counter the ever-increasing slave population, the quarantine of smallpox victims and the Free School Act, which provided governmental assistance to the parishes for education. The Proprietors declared Gibbes's election illegal because of bribery and refused to pay his salary. Charles Craven was appointed his replacement.[22]

The last proprietary governor, James Moore Jr., had a career similar to his father's. He was an Indian fighter who helped break the might of the Tuscarora Indians (1711–13). He returned home and later commanded the provincial forces that put down the Yemassee Indians. Although his leadership was credited with helping to save the colony, once the Indian threat was eliminated, the Proprietors removed him as commander of the provincial forces because of his opposition to their views. Moore was elected to serve as governor during the transition between the proprietary regime and the arrival of the first royal governor in 1721. He was Speaker of the House when he died in 1724.[23]

By the time Arthur Middleton (1681–1737) became governor, the Goose Creek men had finally rid the colony of proprietary rule. Middleton inherited property from his father, Edward Middleton, in the Carolinas as well as in Barbados and England. He inherited three settled Carolina plantations and made The Oaks in Goose Creek Parish, his principal residence (1,630 acres and sixty slaves to run it). He also owned almost eight thousand acres of

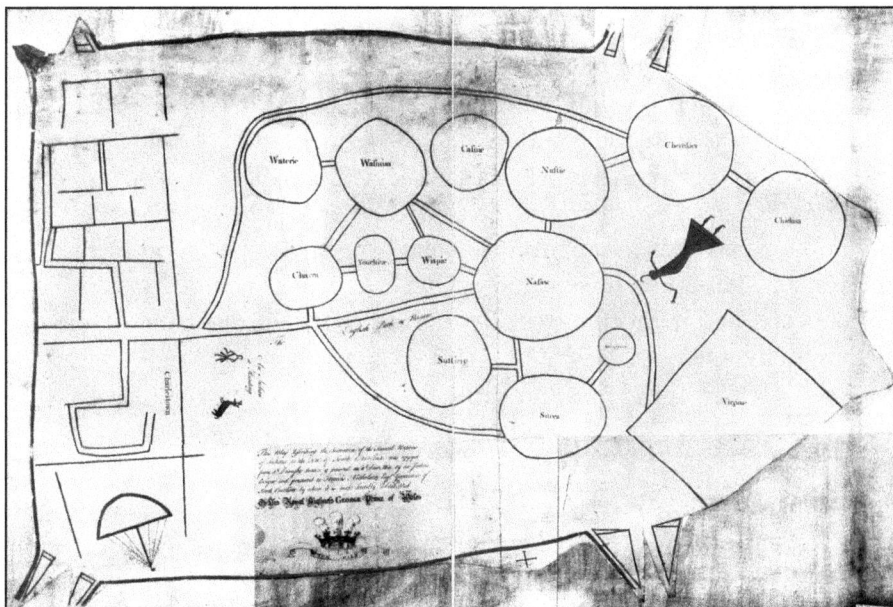

"This map describing the scituation [sic] of several nations of Indians to the NW of South Carolina was coppyed [sic] from a draught & painted on a deer skin by an Indian Cacique and presented to Francis Nicholson, Esqr, governor of south Carolina by whom it is most humbly dedicated to his royal Highness George, Prince of Wales." *Courtesy Library of Congress.*

undeveloped land and a Charles Towne town house. Middleton served in numerous capacities, and while a member of the Grand Council, he was sent to Virginia to seek aid in the Yemassee War.

Upset over proprietary mismanagement, Middleton resigned from the Council and was elected to three terms in the General Assembly, where he signed petitions urging the overthrow of the ruling regime. He was elected president of the new Royal Council and, as such, went on to become acting governor of South Carolina (1724–29) after Governor Nicholson left the province.

Middleton apparently lacked the tact necessary for high office. He was accused of selling public offices for his personal benefit and had numerous confrontations with the Commons House because of his refusal to recognize the House's selection of clerk, his delaying of orders from England and his opposition to the issuing of paper currency.

When Landgrave Thomas Smith tried to restore confidence in the government by assuming the presidency, Middleton had him arrested for treason. Smith's followers were joined by the local militia and marched to Charles Town, causing fear of civil strife. Middleton was replaced by Robert Johnson in 1730.

Middleton remained on the Royal Council and, through that position, acquired 9,579 acres of land, more acreage than he was legally permitted. Although he was extremely wealthy, he had the reputation of being a miser.[24]

Those early settlers have been described as men who "do not inspire us with great regard for their characters generally, or lead us to believe that they were other than such as might have been expected to be found in such an enterprise. They were adventurers whom one cause or another—domestic or political—had induced to seek in the New World fortunes they could not achieve in the Old."[25]

✳✳✳

The Lords Proprietor granted Sir John Yeamans's plantation to his widow, Lady Margaret Yeamans. Her daughter, Margaret Berringer, married Governor Moore, and their daughter, Margaret, married Thomas Smith, landgrave and a governor of Carolina (1693–94).

The original Yeamans dwelling was replaced by a new house built by Landgrave Thomas Smith II in 1695. The plantation was called Goose

The Goose Creek Men

St. James Goose Creek. *Courtesy College of Charleston Special Collections Library, Waddell Collection, Charleston, South Carolina.*

Creek after the nearby body of water. In the mid-nineteenth century, one of Landgrave Smith's descendants renovated and renamed the mansion after the first owners. Only Smith's family members ever lived in the Goose Creek mansion. The earthquake of 1886 made it uninhabitable, and it burned down several years later.

Yeamans Hall remained in the Smith family until the twentieth century, when it became a winter colony for wealthy northerners. The master plan was put together by Frederick Law Olmsted Jr., son of the landscape architect who planned New York's Central Park. It included 250 houses, two eighteen-hole golf courses and a hotel. Due to the Great Depression, what actually got built was a gated community with far fewer houses and a single golf course designed by Seth Raynor, a 1920s designer of high-society clubs. The clubhouse and quadrangles of cottages designed by James Gamble Rogers, architect of the Yale Club in New York City, are still in use.

Nearby is St. James Goose Creek Church, where a tablet bears the inscription:

25

To perpetuate the Memory of
Edward Middleton, Esq.
Who arrived in the Province of South Carolina in the year 1678
Settled at the "Oaks" near this Church
Was of the Grand Council of Carolina.
Died in 1685
And of his Son
The Honorable Arthur Middleton
For many years President of His Majesty's Council in
and Commander in Chief of, the Province of South Carolina
Born in South Carolina in 1681
Died 7ᵗʰ September, 1737
And of the latter's Son
The Honorable Henry Middleton
A member of his Majesty's Council, & thereafter a President
Of the first Continental Congress in 1774
A member of the Council of Safety and President of the
Provincial Congress in South Carolina in 1775–1776
Born in 1717–Died 13ᵗʰ June, 1784
And of his Son
Thomas Middleton Esq.
A member of the Commons House of Assembly of the Province, and
Thereafter of the Provincial Congress
Born 26ᵗʰ July, 1753–Died 19ᵗʰ August, 1797
The last three of whom were residents of this Parish, and each
For many years of the Vestry of this Church: and rest as to
Their earthly part without the Eastern wall of this
Church Adjacent to the Chancel
Memoris nostra durabit si vita meruimus.

GENTLEMEN'S PURSUITS

The practice of charitable societies started shortly after Carolina became a royal crown colony in 1719. Charles Town's leading citizens recognized a need to assist their less fortunate countrymen, and they certainly liked the conviviality afforded by their clubs.

The St. Andrew's Society of Charleston was founded in 1729 to provide relief for the indigent. Its organizers were mainly gentlemen of Scottish descent, but membership quickly grew to include other prominent citizens. In 1814, the society built a handsome hall on Broad Street that was designed by Hugh Smith. Not only was it the headquarters of the St. Andrew's Society, it was also used for meetings of the South Carolina Jockey Club and the St. Cecilia Society. It was a gathering place for balls, concerts and other aspects of the social life of Charleston's elite. Both President James Monroe and General Marquis de Lafayette stayed there. In December 1860, delegates from South Carolina met there to discuss secession. The popular meeting place was destroyed in the Fire of 1861.

The South Carolina Society was founded in 1737 by Huguenots who collected funds for the relief of their countrymen. They soon took in prominent English, Scots-Irish and Scots as members and started educating orphans as early as 1740. The organization continued to prosper and, in 1804, built an imposing meeting hall that was intended to be both a school and a social hall. Designed by Charleston's "gentleman" architect, Gabriel Manigault, the building is now recognized as one of the finest examples of Federal architecture in the nation. (The portico designed by Frederick Wesner was added in 1825).

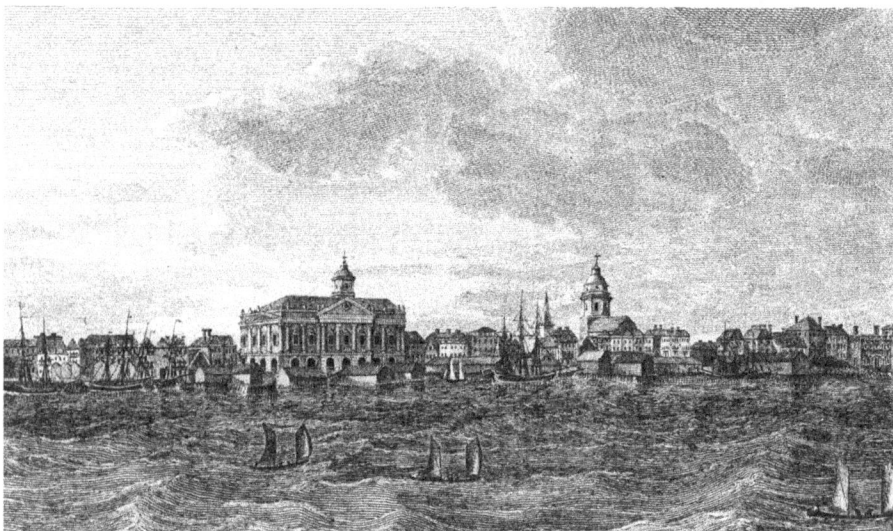

A View of Charles Town, the Capital of South Carolina...in the Year 1774 detail from painting by Thomas Leitch, engraved by Samuel Smith, 1774. *Courtesy College of Charleston Special Collections Library, Waddell Collection, Charleston, South Carolina.*

St. George's Society was founded in 1733 in honor of the patron saint of England, and in 1766 the German Friendly Society was formed with a mission to pay sick and death benefits and to provide resources for low-interest loans. Membership was not limited to Germans. After the earthquake of 1886, it purchased and remodeled the Charleston Bible Society repository at 29 Chalmers Street.

By 1801, the Hibernian Society was established to aid Irish immigrants. In the 1830s, the society's members bought a lot on Meeting Street and hired the eminent Philadelphia architect Thomas U. Walter, famous for the Capitol dome, to design an imposing building that showcased the very latest architectural style.

Although many of these organizations continue to meet, the exclusive Jockey Club of South Carolina disbanded after the Civil War, and the Charleston Bible Society no longer enjoys the prominence it once had.

THE JOCKEY CLUB OF SOUTH CAROLINA

Like true Englishmen, the early Carolinians were devoted to field sports and rode horses from their infancy. Children learned to ride on tackies, which were the size of ponies. Horses were trained to excel in two gaits:

Hibernian Hall, Thomas U. Walter, architect. *Courtesy Charleston Museum, Charleston, South Carolina.*

the canter and the walk. The saddle horses were hunters, and because the terrain was unsuited for fox hunting, deer hunting was the great local sport. Hunts were carried on once or twice a month by social clubs that delighted in their horses, hounds and guns. Afterward the hunters would meet in a plain building, called a clubhouse, for dinner. The clubhouse in St. Andrew's Parish was built in 1761.

Virginia was the main supplier of horses to the early province. They were imported in such great numbers that as early as 1700 the Assembly had passed an importation tax to encourage breeding horses locally.

In addition to Virginia-bred horses, plantation owners rode horses of the Chickasaw breed that were supposed to be descended from the barbs left by the early Spanish discoverers. These horses had been introduced into Spain by the Arabs and were noted for their speed and endurance. Although small, barbs were fine racers and hunters, and by mid-century planters were crossbreeding them with imported thoroughbreds. These thoroughbreds often had impressive bloodlines. The principal horse breeders were Thomas Nightingale, Daniel Ravenel, Edward and Nicholas Harleston, Francis Huger and William Middleton.[26]

In 1734, the *South Carolina Gazette* published notice of the first public race—the prize was a saddle and bridle valued at twenty pounds. The race took place on Charles Town's Neck, opposite a public house known as Bowling Green House.

In 1735, a more formal course, named after the fashionable course in York, England, was laid out about six miles from town.[27]

Because of the inconvenient distance of the York course, a new course was established by subscription in 1754. Just a mile from town, it was announced as the New Market Course, and races started six years later. The course was located on the Blake Tract and occupied the ground between King Street and the low ground of the Cooper River, as Meeting Street had not yet been laid out.

By 1758, horse racing had attained such popularity that the gentlemen of the turf founded the South Carolina Jockey Club, the first such organization in the colonies. The first race producing unusual excitement was a four-mile match at the New Market Course held on the last day of January 1769, between William Henry Drayton's Carolina-bred horse, Adolphus, and Thomas Nightingale's imported horse, Shadow. The imported horse had been bred by Lord Northumberland and won handily. There were other pricy celebrity horses, including Flimnap, imported by Mansell, Corbett & Company, of Charlestown, which beat all of the other horses in the country, including one owned by Mr. Nightingale.

It was not long before the Jockey Club's races became the premier events of the social season. Only gentlemen were permitted to ride. They did not run for the money but rather for the "honor" that a horse brought its owner. Originally, the purses were silver plate in order to remove all vulgarity from the sport.[28]

Edward Fenwick, one of the eight original founders of the Jockey Club, maintained a three-and-a-half-mile racetrack at his home on Johns Island. In England, Fenwick was known as the "Founder of the Turf in Carolina."[29]

As war loomed on the horizon, in 1774 the Continental Congress introduced "Articles of Association" in which frivolous entertainments were suppressed. The offense of horse racing included a hefty fine and forfeiture of the horse. This was not a hardship for New Englanders, who did not engage in horse racing, but it greatly affected Virginians and Carolinians.

During the Revolution, some of the most sought-after spoils of war were thoroughbred horses, and there are wonderful tales of how these thefts were foiled. One anecdote is about Wantoot in St. John's Parish. The owner, Daniel Ravenel, was away at war and left a slave overseer in charge of the plantation. When he overheard that the British intended to steal the horse, the ingenious overseer crafted a plan. He removed

Fenwick Hall, once home of Edward Fenwick, "Founder of the Turf in Carolina." *Courtesy Charleston Museum, Charleston, South Carolina.*

the floorboards in his tiny house to muffle any noise that might be made by the horse's hooves and concealed the horse inside. When the British demanded to know the horse's whereabouts, he was afraid that it would neigh. Maintaining his composure, he informed the British soldiers that he knew nuttin' 'bout de hos'. In recounting the tale to the family later, he "tanked de Lord w'en dem British gone. He nearly kill heself with de laf at foolin' dem British."[30]

Repeated efforts to get the celebrated Flimnap, then owned by Major Isaac Harleston, were unsuccessful primarily through the faithfulness of Negro grooms. Because he would not reveal the concealment of the horse, one groom was actually hanged and left for dead by a detachment of British troops. He was later cut down and recovered. Upon Harleston's death in 1783, the groom who had saved Flimnap was given his freedom and a lifelong residence and pension to prevent his being a burden on society.[31]

Activities of the Jockey Club were suspended during the conflict but were almost immediately back in operation the year after the British evacuated Charles Town. General John McPherson, General Wade Hampton, Colonel William Alston, Colonel Washington and Arthur Middleton were among the "gentlemen of the turf" who spearheaded the renewed interest in horse racing.[32] The Jockey Club was forced to disband twice during the next twenty years because of economic problems after the war.

The nineteenth century ushered in what has become nostalgically known as the "Golden Age of Racing." Race Week quickly became the highlight of the South Carolina social season. It was planned with the same enthusiasm

By particular Request of the Members

OF THE

JOCKEY-CLUB.

THIS EVENING, SATURDAY, FEBRUARY, 23, 1805,

Will be Presented the Musical Drama, interspersed with Songs, Chorusses, &c. Called the

Mountaineers.

OCTAVIAN,	Mr. HODGKINSON,	BULCAZIN MULLY,	Mr. TURNBULL,
VIROLET,	Mr. STORY,	GANEM,	Mr. BARRYMORE,
KILMALLOCK,	Mr. BARRETT,	ROQUE,	Mr. RUTHERFORD,
SADI,	Mr. SULLY,	OLD GOATHERD,	Mr. BERNARD,
LOPE TOCHO,	Mr. DYKES,	GOATHERD'S SON,	Mr. LINDSLEY.
ZORAYDA,	Mrs. PLACIDE,	AGNES,	Mrs. MARSHALL,
FLORANTHE,	Mrs. VILLIERS,		

Muleteers & Goatherds, Melica Clarnock, Harman, Weil, Barrymore, and Wilson.

Female Villagers, Mrs. &c. Marshall, Miss Field, Mrs. Dykes, &c.

To which will be added, the Grand Dramatic ROMANCE, called

Blue Beard;

OR,

Female Curiosity.

Written by George Coleman, the younger; and performed upwards of one hundred and fifty Nights, at the Theatre-Royal, Drury-Lane, London: With additional Scenery, Machinery, and Decorations: The Music composed and selected by Mr. Kelly, the Orchestra accompaniments, by Mr. Leaumont.

ABOMELIQUE,	(Blue Beard)	Mr. RUTHERFORD,	FATIMA,	(Betrothed to Blue Beard)	Mrs. MARSHALL,
IBRAHIM,		Mr. WILMOT,	IRENE,	(Sister of Fatima)	Miss FIELD,
SELIM,	(Lover of Fatima)	Mr. STORY,	BEDA,		Mrs. VILLIERS,
SHACABAC,		Mr. SULLY,			

ACT I.—A View of a TURKISH VILLAGE; and a grand Procession
of ABOMELIQUE, Seated on an

ELEPHANT;

And his TRAIN, to claim his intended BRIDE.

ACT II.—A BLUE MAGIC CHAMBER,

Superbly decorated in the EASTERN STYLE.

A TURKISH GARDEN, brilliantly and fancifully ILLUMINATED;

With a NUPTIAL FESTIVAL.

The CASTLE of Abomelique; with Turrets, Corridor, Draw-Bridge, &c.

Inside of a SEPULCHRE:—The DEATH of ABOMELIQUE.

Courtesy Charleston Museum, Charleston, South Carolina.

as Mardi Gras in New Orleans and Carnival in Rio. People came from all over the state. All business was suspended, and the whole community joined in a time of "hospitality, merriment and open-heartedness, bringing round an epoch of social delight…a happy state of companionship and mutual good-will."[33]

It was said that the gentlemen seemed to regret even the necessity of sleep and longed for the morning to renew their pleasures. Races started the first Wednesday of February and were followed by a lively members' banquet that evening. Races continued for the next two days and culminated with the Jockey Club's "ball of all balls" on Friday evening. The club's activities were compressed into only one week a year as members felt that their pleasures were "higher when rarely used."[34]

In 1836, the Jockey Club built the elegant Washington Race Course (currently the site of Hampton Park), complete with four handsome stone pillars at the entrance. The reviewing stand was designed by Charles Reichardt, a German architect who had arrived in Charleston in 1836 with considerable fanfare. He let it be known that he was a favorite pupil of the Prussian architect Karl Freidrich Schinkel, considered to be the greatest German architect of the time. With that recommendation, Reichardt was able to land some of the most prestigious contracts in the city.

The reviewing stand was a great success. With easy access to the field for the gentlemen, it boasted a covered entrance and carpeted retiring rooms for

The racecourse clubhouse (demolished), Charles F. Reichardt, architect. *Courtesy Library of Congress.*

the ladies. There were even complimentary public stands for spectators who were not part of the aristocracy.

Due to the popularity of Race Week, the prestigious St. Cecilia Society decided to change its annual elections from February to November, and it suspended all musical entertainments during that week.[35]

South Carolina's cherished "Golden Age of Racing" abruptly ended with the advent of the Civil War. The Jockey Club never recovered its former glory and disbanded on December 28, 1899, donating the race course and adjoining farmland to the Charleston Library Society.[36] Although the clubhouse has not survived, the four stone pillars that graced the entrance of the race course were donated by Charleston's City Fathers to Belmont Park on Long Island when it opened in 1905.[37]

THE CHARLESTON BIBLE SOCIETY

With membership that included some of the city's most distinguished citizens, it was logical that when the Charleston Bible Society organized on June 11, 1810, it met at the newly built South Carolina Hall on lower Meeting Street.

The society's founders followed a tradition started in 1804 by the British and Foreign Bible Society in London, which had the ambitious goal of distributing Bibles throughout the world. The United States did not take long to follow suit. Started in 1806, the Philadelphia Bible Society was the first to be established in America. It was followed by Bible societies in Massachusetts, Connecticut and Maine. The Charleston Bible Society is the fifth oldest in the nation and shares with the Maryland Bible Society the 1810 founding date.

The Charleston Bible Society wanted to encourage a study of the Holy Scriptures and was ecumenical from the very beginning. The first planning meeting was presided over by Thomas Lowndes, brother of Congressman William Lowndes. Attorney William Hasell Gibbes, who attended St. Philips,

South Carolina Hall, Gabriel Manigault, architect. *Courtesy Charleston Museum, Charleston, South Carolina.*

took the minutes. The committee chosen to draft the society's constitution consisted of an impressive group of clergymen: Reverend Dr. Isaac Stockton Keith, Reverend William Percy, Reverend Richard Furman and Father Simon Felix Gallagher.

The pastor of the enormous Circular Congregational Church, Reverend Dr. Keith, was a distinguished scholar and Princeton graduate who had come from the Presbyterian church in Alexandria, Virginia. The Reverend William Percy had just established St. Paul's, the third Episcopal church in the city.

When Richard Furman volunteered to fight in the Revolution, Governor John Rutledge persuaded him to convert Loyalists to the Patriot cause in the western part of the state. He was so successful that the British commander, Lord Cornwallis, was said to have feared his fiery prayers "more than the armies of Marion and Sumter."[38]

Father Simon Felix Gallagher, a native of Dublin, was the longtime pastor of St. Mary's Church, the first Catholic church in Charleston. Active in civic affairs, he helped establish the Hibernian Society and was on the faculty of the College of Charleston, where he helped enhance rigorous scholarship at the fledgling institution. He was considered a brilliant wit and a friendly drinking companion. Gallagher's actions kept him in the center of trouble to the extent that he was temporarily suspended from his duties as punishment for riotous partying with parish trustees.[39]

Lay members chosen to draft the constitution were John Bull, Robert Dewar and Timothy Ford. Another committee was charged to obtain subscriptions, receive money and present a report at next meeting. When the society met the following month, there were 275 subscribers and $2,296 had been collected. They elected General Charles Cotesworth Pinckney as president.

Pinckney was the son of colonial Chief Justice Charles Pinckney and Eliza Lucas Pinckney. He was educated in England at the prestigious Westminster School, went on to Oxford University and studied law at the Middle Temple. He continued his education in France before returning to the colonies. In 1773, he married Sarah Middleton, whose brother, Arthur, signed the Declaration of Independence.

Long recognized as one of the Founding Fathers, Pinckney served as a brigadier general in the Continental army and was a personal friend of George Washington. He also signed the U.S. Constitution. He was minister to France and represented the new nation in the famous "XYZ" Affair in which he allegedly said, "Millions for defense, Sir, but not one d----d penny for tribute." He ran unsuccessfully as the Federalist candidate for vice president in 1800 and for president in 1804 and 1808. He was a founder of South Carolina College, now the University of South Carolina. He was also president of the South Carolina Jockey Club, president of the Society for Relief of Widows and Orphans, president of the Charleston Library Society and president of the Society of the Cincinnati of the State of South Carolina.[40]

The Bible Society vice-presidents were an equally impressive array of clergy: the Reverend Dr. Keith, Reverend Furman, Reverend Percy, and the Right Reverend Theodore Dehon, second Protestant

Charles Cotesworth Pinckney. *Courtesy Charleston Museum, Charleston, South Carolina.*

Episcopal bishop of South Carolina, who married Nathaniel Russell's daughter, Sarah, in 1813. The corresponding secretaries were Reverend Andrew Flinn and the Right Reverend Christopher Gadsden, the fourth Episcopal bishop of South Carolina.

Recording secretary was Timothy Ford from Morristown, New Jersey. During the Revolution, the Ford mansion had been General George Washington's headquarters from December 1779 to June 1780. That summer, young Ford volunteered with Washington's Life Guard at Connecticut Farms, where he was wounded. He started Princeton that fall, later graduated and studied law under Robert Morris in New York.

When Timothy Ford's sister, Elizabeth, married William De Saussure, he accompanied them to Charleston and becomes a partner in De Saussure's law firm. Ford built a house on lower Meeting Street where he entertained the Marquis de Lafayette during his visit to Charleston in 1824.

The first treasurer was Nathaniel Russell, a highly successful merchant from Rhode Island who was twenty-seven when he came to Charleston and amassed a huge fortune. Across Meeting Street from Timothy Ford's home, Russell built a town house that is recognized today as one of America's most

Ford Mansion (General George Washington's 1779–80 winter headquarters in Morristown, New Jersey). *Courtesy Dr. and Mrs. Bert Pruitt.*

Number 54 Meeting Street. *Courtesy Dr. and Mrs. Bert Pruitt.*

Rear view of 54 Meeting, with Nathaniel Russell House and First Scots Presbyterian Church in the background. *Courtesy Dr. and Mrs. Bert Pruitt.*

important Neoclassical dwellings. He was a member of the Congregational Church. (Russell's wife was a member of St. Michael's and founded, with her two daughters and sister, the Ladies Benevolent Society, which provided basic necessities to the indigent; it later became the first visiting nurses program in the nation.)[41]

The first meetings were held at the College of Charleston, but by 1828 there were sufficient funds to construct a two-story repository at 29 Chalmers Street, where the society remained until the earthquake of 1886 severely damaged the building. The repository was moved several times before relocating to Second Presbyterian Church on Meeting Street.

In 1970, the society's leather-bound minutes were discovered in a safe in one of the former repositories, Siegling's Music House. Dated 1851–1905, the old-fashioned handwritten ledger told an extraordinary story.

The greatest emergency came in 1861, when the organization began supplying Bibles to Confederate troops. A week after the attack on Fort Sumter, President Lincoln called for a blockade of Confederate ports. No longer able to buy Bibles from Northern printers, the society obtained some from Nashville, long a printer of Bibles. Eight cases of Bibles were shipped directly from London, and five thousand Bibles came into port via blockade runners from Nassau; the cost was underwritten by Fraser, Trenholm and Company, the most successful blockade runners of them all.[42]

The Confederacy's first New Testament was published by Wood, Hanleiter Rice and Company in Atlanta. The three- by five-and-a-half-inch size of the Bibles made them easy for soldiers to carry.

The war led to the establishment of the Bible Society of the Confederate States in Orangeburg, South Carolina. One of the men who played a role in the beginning of the Confederate Bible Society was a Presbyterian minister, Reverend Joseph Ruggles Wilson. His son, Woodrow, would become the twenty-eighth president of the United States. In 1865, when the war was nearing its end, Charleston was able to resume contact with the American Bible Society, which had given more than 300,000 volumes to Southern armies and civilians.[43]

The Charleston Bible Society also provided one thousand Bibles for men fighting in the Spanish-American War. Over the years, recipients have been merchant seamen, orphanages, churches, jails, immigrants, homeless shelters, foreign mission teams, the blind and military personnel. The society continues to meet to fulfill the mission of its founders.[44]

***

The Bible may not have changed much, but worship in Charleston has. As Reverend Doctor A. Toomer Porter described:

> *The Clergy wore black gowns to preach in, with long white bands around their necks. Men did not kneel in church; it was very funny to see them come in and put their faces into their beaver hats, for a second or two, to say a preparatory prayer, I suppose. The offerings were taken up in the hats of the wardens and the vestry, standing by each door with a white pocket-handkerchief thrown over the hat. When a corpse was taken up the aisle, all the pallbearers made a table of the coffin and put their hats on it...The first time the* Te Deum *was sung at Saint Michael's Church, I remember the commotion was so great that one might have thought the whole of St. Michael's Church, steeple and all, had gone bodily into the Church of Rome...It was very bad manners to join in the hymn, and to respond to the service was vulgar. One wonders how the Episcopal Church ever survived such misuse of its liturgy and neglect of these privileges. The Holy Communion was administered (to have spoken of a celebration would have been heresy) on the first Sunday of the month, and the whole congregation left, save a small remnant of dear old ladies, and some decrepit men...the congregation departing with the major benediction.*[45]

THE DRAYTONS OF DRAYTON HALL

THE COLONIALS

The Carolina settlers were capable men who quickly patterned a lifestyle similar to the Caribbean colonial model. Within thirty years of their arrival, an early English surveyor commented that colonists "were a genteel sort of people that were all acquainted with the trade, and had either money or parts to make good use of the advantages that offered as most have done by raising themselves to great estates…The gentlemen seated in the country are very courteous, live very nobly in their houses, and give very genteel entertainments to all strangers and others that come to visit them."[46]

The Ashley River had been the site of the first settlement, and by the 1740s its left bank was graced with stately homes built by some of the first families of the Province: Bulls, Bakers, Draytons, Godfreys, Linings, Middletons, Savages, Warings and Woodwards. The river became the commercial highway, and people traveled into town in canoes manned by skilled slave oarsmen.

St. Andrew's Parish had one of the first roads in the province. It ran parallel to the river, about half a mile inland, beginning where the Wappoo met the Ashley and meandered up to Bacon's Bridge at Old Dorchester. An avenue from each plantation led out to the road, which was maintained by the local landowners.

In the early days, when the gentry visited by land, the men sometimes rode spirited barbs, and their ladies accompanied them in chaises. Today, of all the beautiful Ashley River homes, only three names remain part of local iconography: Middleton Place, once home of a signer of the Declaration of Independence, and two Drayton residences, Magnolia and Drayton Hall. Of those, only Drayton Hall, the home of Charles Drayton, survived the ravages of the Civil War.[47]

According to family records, Thomas Drayton Jr., also known as "Thomas the Immigrant," was the progenitor of the Drayton family in South Carolina. He emigrated from Barbados in 1679 on the ship *Mary* along with Stephen and Phillis Fox. When he arrived in Carolina, Stephen Fox purchased a 402-acre tract in St. Andrew's Parish on the Ashley River. His daughter, Ann Fox, inherited the land, and her husband, Thomas Drayton, built Magnolia. He raised cattle, and as he prospered, he acquired more land and more slaves. He became part of the planter aristocracy, and by the time of his death, he had an estate that comprised several plantations, more than 1,300 head of cattle, about 150 horses and forty-six slaves. In 1717, Thomas Drayton III, his oldest son, inherited the property, as primogeniture was the custom of the day. The practice derived from English law whereby the eldest son inherited all of the real estate to the exclusion of any other children. Younger sons were expected to go into the professions, military or church and, it was hoped, to marry well.

John Drayton, Thomas's third son, purchased 350 acres just south of his father's plantation. John married four times. His first wife and their two children died. In 1742, John married Charlotta Bull, daughter of Royal Lieutenant Governor William Bull. They had two sons, William Henry and Charles. Upon his second wife's death, he married Margaret Glen, sister of Royal Governor James Glen. They, too, had two sons, Glen and Thomas. Margaret died in 1772, and three years later John married Rebecca Perry, the seventeen-year-old daughter of a neighbor. They had three children.

As a younger son, John Drayton worked hard to establish himself. He was only twenty-three when he began to make the transition from ranching to rice planting. This was a laborious and time-consuming commitment, even with labor provided by the enslaved people who performed the plantation's daily tasks. Like his father before him, he prospered and built Drayton Hall a mere seventy years after the Carolina colony was founded. The manor house was designed in a modified Palladian style derived from popular architectural design books such as that of James Gibbs.

Shortly after the mansion was completed in 1742, Drayton built a garden house that was intended to be used for entertaining. Facing the main house, it is one of the oldest-known structures of its kind in the South. The surviving brickwork recently uncovered in archaeological digs illustrates

The Draytons of Drayton Hall

Pierre Eugene Du Simitiere (circa 1736–1784), *Drayton Hall S.C.* Dated "1765" on reverse. Watercolor, pencil and ink on laid paper, 8 ³/₈ x 12 ¹/₂ inches. *Private collection, courtesy the owner, Jim Lockard.*

the importance that Drayton attached to the design. Between the Ashley River and the main house was an English-style garden. The land side of the mansion was equally impressive, especially when flanker buildings completed the complex. In 1758, an advertisement for the sale of a plantation across the river specifically mentioned that the property held "an agreeable prospect of John Drayton's palace and gardens."

An industrious man, John Drayton managed his own estate and enjoyed being a member of the close-knit planter aristocracy. He had a passion for horses and was one of the eight founders of the elite South Carolina Jockey Club. Allied with the royal government, he rose through the ranks until he became a member of the Royal Governor's Council. He supported the enforcement of the unpopular Stamp Act of 1765 and the equally detested Tea Act of 1773 that enabled the financially beleaguered East India Company to sell tea to a few favored agents in each colony.[48]

The Tea Act not only precipitated the Boston Tea Party but also met great resistance in Charles Town, where irate citizens had their own "tea party." On November 3, 1774, amid the cheers of a boisterous crowd ashore, three favored tea consignees were forced to dump chests of valuable tea from a boat into Charleston Harbor during a mock "Oblation to Neptune."[49]

Like others of the planter aristocracy, John Drayton sent his sons to England to acquire the manners to deport themselves as gentlemen. They studied the classics and learned the arts of dancing, fencing and playing a musical instrument. They quickly learned that, in spite of their elite colonial social position, in England they were merely "gentleman commoners," ranking below noblemen and aristocrats and only slightly above lowly merchants' sons.

The most famous of John Drayton's children was William Henry Drayton (1742–1779), his son by Charlotta Bull. In 1753, the youngster was sent to England to complete his education. He traveled under the watchful care of former chief justice Charles Pinckney and his wife, Eliza Lucas. After attending the fashionable Westminster School for eight years of rigorous study, young Drayton attended Balliol College, Oxford. He apparently enjoyed a frivolous student lifestyle, for he ran up large debts. His father refused to honor them and called him home. The following year, young Drayton married one of the wealthiest heiresses in the colony, Dorothy Golightly; the couple settled in St. Bartholomew's Parish on property his wife inherited. Like his father, he had a passion for racehorses and maintained a stable of thoroughbreds that was managed by white employees.

William Henry Drayton (1742–1779), one of the Founding Fathers, was inducted into South Carolina Hall of Fame in 2006. *Courtesy Drayton Hall.*

Ambitious, fabulously wealthy and well connected with the royal government, Drayton sought public office. Lack of experience and continued gambling debts caused him to be regarded as a dilettante who was clearly out of his element. His early political career was described by one historian as a "fiasco." After he failed to be reelected to the Royal Assembly, he published a polemic in the *South Carolina Gazette* decrying the opponents of the Townshend Duties. These duties were as unpopular as the 1764 Stamp Act.

Feisty Christopher Gadsden, a wealthy merchant and self-proclaimed hero of the Stamp Act Congress, took issue with Drayton, and the two men engaged in a five-month newspaper debate. This was young Drayton's mistake. His unpopular stance caused him to become an anathema to the non-importation faction. They ostracized him both socially and economically. Christopher Gadsden had a one-thousand-foot wharf described as a "stupendous work…which is reckoned as the most extensive of its kind ever undertaken by any one man in America."[50] Gadsden and his friends boycotted Drayton, forcing him to market his own rice in London at a great disadvantage. Politically, Drayton failed to be appointed to a judgeship—even with the recommendation of his uncle, Lieutenant Governor William Bull.

Hoping to be better received in England, Drayton sailed back in 1770. To gain favor, he published *The Letters of a Freeman* (a recap of his newspaper series) and obtained an introduction at court. After he was able to secure an appointment to the South Carolina Royal Council, he returned to the colony.

No one knows for sure why William Henry Drayton had a radical political transformation, but once back home, he soon abandoned his impassioned support of the Crown. He began to rail against British authority to such an extent that he was suspended from the Royal Council in 1774.

Once he changed his tune, he and Gadsden became fast friends. His political ranting caused him to be elected to the First South Carolina Provincial Congress, representing the Saxe Gotha District. After obtaining a treaty of neutrality from backcountry pro-British sympathizers, he was elected chairman of the Second Provincial Congress. In that capacity, Drayton oversaw the formation of South Carolina's first constitution.

Drayton personally went on board the *Defense* to oversee the execution of harbor defenses. Hoping to provoke an incident, on November 11, 1775, Drayton ordered the *Defense* to return the fire of the British warship *Tamar*, thus initiating hostilities in the Carolinas. Although citizens welcomed the *Defense* back to port amid loud cheers, Rawlins Lowndes and other more conservative statesmen feared that radical young hotheads would provoke war with mighty England.[51]

Drayton served as chief justice of South Carolina from 1775 to 1779 and was appointed to the Second Continental Congress in Philadelphia in 1778. A tireless worker, he served on numerous ad hoc committees and five of the eight standing committees. He was writing a history of the Revolution when he died of typhoid fever in 1779; he was buried at Christ Church in Philadelphia.

Upon Drayton's death, a Charleston newspaper wrote, "[T]he American States have lost one of their principal supporters, and posterity may regret that his fate prevented him from exerting his great talents towards organizing this new world into a great, happy, and flourishing empire." Today William Henry Drayton is considered one of the country's Founding Fathers and one of its most effective polemicists.[52]

The same year that William Henry Drayton died in Philadelphia, British troops arrived at Drayton Hall for the first time. The aging John Drayton, Rebecca, his young fourth wife, and three small children evacuated before the advancing army. While crossing the Cooper River at Strawberry Ferry, John Drayton suffered a fatal seizure. He was buried in an unmarked grave.

The following year, Sir Henry Clinton commandeered the plantation as field headquarters for several thousand troops. Six days later, the British crossed the Ashley River to lay siege to Charles Town. That summer, General Cornwallis quartered his troops at Drayton Hall and remained there until the British evacuated. Colonial General "Mad" Anthony Wayne then moved in and used the plantation for his headquarters. By the time the war was over, the ornamental gardens and numerous outbuildings had been completely destroyed; only the mansion had survived intact.

SUCCEEDING GENERATIONS

In 1784, widowed Rebecca Drayton sold Drayton Hall to her stepson (William Henry's younger brother), Charles Drayton (1743–1820), the eldest surviving son of John Drayton. He continued his father's multifaceted fascination with scientific investigation. His extensive writings, dating from 1784 to 1820, are full of commentary on botany, architecture, landscape design, animal husbandry and design efficiencies. Charles Drayton conducted weather experiments, read about the latest discoveries and devoted considerable time to agriculture. He also grew cotton and built the necessary structures to support its cultivation. In 1802, he made the first major change to the main house by replacing three Georgian mantels on the first floor with Federal (or Adam) mantels. He was one of the first people in America to convert traditional open fireplaces into the more efficient Rumford fireboxes.

Charles Drayton transformed the remnants of his father's eighteenth-century garden into the newly fashionable *ferme ornée* (ornamental farm). Popular in France and England, the style blended functionality and aesthetics. Wishing to enjoy the sweeping view of the Ashley River, he constructed a ha-ha, a sunken barrier that kept sheep and other livestock in grazing areas away from the riverfront formal gardens. He also installed ponds that were used to hold fish for domestic consumption.

The Draytons of Drayton Hall

Drayton was a friend of André Michaux, the French botanist and explorer who introduced the ginkgo tree and other exotic plants to the Lowcountry. Michaux maintained a base in Charleston for ten years while he made expeditions to catalogue indigenous flora. Drayton also corresponded with Thomas Jefferson. While Jefferson was minister to France, he sent Drayton 118 olive stones growing in dirt. Unfortunately, the climate was too harsh, and the olive seedling experiment failed.

Upon his death, his son, Charles Drayton II, inherited Drayton Hall. He, in turn, left the plantation to his son, Charles Drayton III, who was only thirty-eight when he died. Charles Drayton III left Drayton Hall to his oldest son, Charles Henry Drayton (1852–1915), when he was just five years old. During Charles Henry Drayton's minority, his uncle, Dr. John Drayton, managed the estate. Dr. Drayton had served in the Confederate cause at many local posts, including James Island, Bee's Ferry and Charleston. In the summer of 1865, after hostilities had ceased, Dr. Drayton returned to Drayton Hall.

There are several theories as to why the mansion survived the Union army's destruction. The Drayton family contends that the most plausible is that Dr. Drayton posted a smallpox notification at the entrance to the property, causing wary troops to give the mansion a wide berth for fear of contracting the dreaded disease.

A contemporary who visited Drayton Hall after the war provided a more colorful explanation, saying that a Union gunboat came up the Ashley River to destroy mansions along the riverbank. According to that account, the Drayton family was dining when they heard the distant volleys. They dashed out of the house, and thinking that all would soon be lost, they fled. The former slave butler got into a log canoe, paddled up to the gunboat and implored the captain not to destroy "Admiral" Drayton's house. According to that account, the house was spared because the Yankee captain did not realize that a fictitious "admiral" did not own Drayton Hall. (Captain Percival Drayton, great grandson of Thomas Jr., had been with the U.S. fleet during the battle of Port Royal; his brother, Confederate general Fenwick Drayton, commanded CSA troops on Hilton Head Island.) Some months later, the Drayton family returned and found their silver and property left untouched; the food had dried on the abandoned dishes.[53]

Dr. Drayton later joined his two brothers in Texas. Before his departure, he set up phosphate mining contracts that his nephew Charles Henry Drayton took over when he came of age. The company operated into the early twentieth century. Charles Henry Drayton built a narrow-gauge railroad and buildings to support the operation. Strip mining took place as close as

Above: Phosphate mining in the 1890s. *Courtesy Charleston Museum, Charleston, South Carolina.*

Right: Drayton Hall, unoccupied. *Courtesy Charleston Museum, Charleston, South Carolina.*

one thousand feet from the main house. Phosphate profits helped the family recover from the losses incurred by the war.

Charles Henry Drayton died in 1915, leaving Drayton Hall to his wife and their three children. By 1926, only two children were still alive, Charles Henry Drayton Jr., and Charlotta Drayton, lovingly referred to by the family youngsters as "Aunt Charley."

Charles Henry Drayton Jr. married the daughter of Admiral Frank E. Beatty, who had retired but was called back to active duty as the commandant of the Sixth Naval District during World War I. Charles Henry Drayton Jr. served in France as a captain in the infantry and earned a bronze medal for bravery. The couple had two sons, Charles (Charlie) Henry Drayton and Francis (Frank) Beatty Drayton (1923–1979).

Charlotta never married and loved spending long periods at her ancestral country home. She never installed plumbing and electricity in the mansion and stipulated in her will that the house remain unchanged.

During the Depression, Henry Francis Du Pont tried to purchase Drayton Hall's great hall woodwork when he was building his extensive decorative

Members of the fifth and sixth generations. *Left to right*: Charles Henry II, Charlotta, Eliza Gantt, Charles Henry I and Eliza. *Courtesy Drayton Hall.*

Drayton Hall in 1890s. *Courtesy Charleston Museum, Charleston, South Carolina.*

arts collection at his ancestral home in Winterthur, Delaware. He was said to have made a very tempting offer, including a replacement of the original woodwork. Preferring to keep the house in its original condition, the Draytons rejected his overture, much to Du Pont's amazement.

PRESERVING A LEGACY

As her brother was already deceased when Charlotta died in 1969, her nephews inherited her share of the property. In the final years of family ownership, Drayton Hall witnessed several candlelit debutante parties, two wedding receptions within six weeks of each other and other special occasions. When the family used the fireplaces, a fire engine was always on hand. Long-ago guests still comment on the lack of indoor plumbing and seeing the fire hoses placed in the well to be prepared in case of an emergency.

Although the aging mansion was occasionally opened to select groups like the Colonial Dames, maintaining the property became increasingly costly. Within five years of ownership, the Drayton brothers came to the reluctant conclusion that they had to take proactive steps to preserve their inheritance. The property was never officially put on the market, but the word got out. A developer made an offer that the brothers promptly rejected when the man revealed that he intended to make the historic mansion a clubhouse for a golf course.

They approached the influential owner of the *News and Courier*, Peter Manigault, who was also a vice-president of the National Trust for Historic Preservation. Manigault arranged for the National Trust to visit Charleston. The demand to see the Georgian-Palladian mansion was so great that it took two days to accommodate everyone. Board members were "quite taken" with the historic property and soon started negotiations. Ultimately, it took three years to complete the transfer.

Frances Edmunds, an esteemed preservationist, got the Historic Charleston Foundation involved. She insisted that a member of the Drayton family always be on the site council. Since its acquisition, the National Trust has

Left to right: George McDaniel, Anne Drayton Nelson, Rebecca Campbell, Charles Drayton, Lorraine White and Catherine Braxton at the program "Share the History, Tell the Story," a special commemoration event at Drayton Hall in 2006. *Courtesy Drayton Hall.*

always kept the Drayton family deeply involved. Family members are invited to functions at Drayton Hall and enjoy an intimate annual Thanksgiving potluck feast under majestic oaks that once witnessed the birth of a nation.

Parting with Drayton Hall after seven generations of continuous ownership was one of the most traumatic experiences of Charlie Drayton's long and productive life. There are no regrets, nor should there be, for with the aggressive housing development in the Lowcountry, few plantations around Charleston have survived urban sprawl.[54]

Conservation along the Ashley River has been subtle. According to the southern landscape historian Suzanne Turner, Drayton Hall has "the most significant, undisturbed historic landscape in America." The scenic river appears serene and peaceful, but it was not always thus.

As people began to prosper after World War II, speedboating on the coastal waterways became a popular sport. By the 1980s and 1990s, speedboats raced along the Ashley, their wakes wearing away the fragile riverbanks. The noise and erosion became such a problem that, under the leadership of Executive Director George McDaniel and Assistant Director George

The Ashley River. *Courtesy Charleston Museum, Charleston, South Carolina.*

Neil, Drayton Hall took the lead and—coordinating with South Carolina Representative Stephen Gonzales, the South Carolina Department of Natural Resources and Middleton Place—successfully secured legislation for "no wake" buoys to be erected along the waterfronts of the sites on the National Register of Historic Places: Drayton Hall, Magnolia Plantation and Gardens, Middleton Place and Colonial Dorchester. This marked the first time that the state designated "no wake" zones solely in order to protect historical resources. In addition, Drayton Hall partnered with the U.S. Army Corps of Engineers and installed two rock abatements to halt erosion of the shoreline.

Urbanization continued its relentless march. In 1994, twenty-five acres of land zoned for twenty-two units per acre came up for sale on the riverbank facing Drayton Hall. A vista of a shopping plaza or high-rise condominiums across the river from Drayton Hall was unimaginable to the many Friends of Drayton Hall. More than one thousand concerned Friends contributed to purchase the land; the seller donated additional acreage along the marsh to ensure the protection of the historic viewshed in perpetuity. In total, Drayton Hall acquired 105 acres through a combination of fundraising and land donations. Afterward, Drayton Hall and the City of North Charleston worked together to obtain a one-hundred-foot vegetation buffer located across the river from National Register properties.[55]

African American Heritage

Drayton Hall has endeavored to preserve the relationship with descendants of the original enslaved Africans who, according to oral history, accompanied Thomas Drayton from Barbados in the 1670s.

Among the most prominent were three siblings—Caesar, John and Catherine—who assumed the name Bowens after freedom. All have numerous descendants living in Charleston and across the nation and are probably buried in the African American cemetery, known as "A Sacred Place," at Drayton Hall. Documented to the 1790s, the cemetery is one of the oldest African American cemeteries in the nation still in use and is open to public visitation. According to family oral history, Catherine Bowens, who married Friday Johnson, was the cook, and their son, Willis Johnson, after growing up at Drayton Hall, "walked to Charleston," worked successfully at a number of jobs and bought land, including the parcel of 35 Calhoun Street near the corner of East Bay, which is still owned by three descendants:

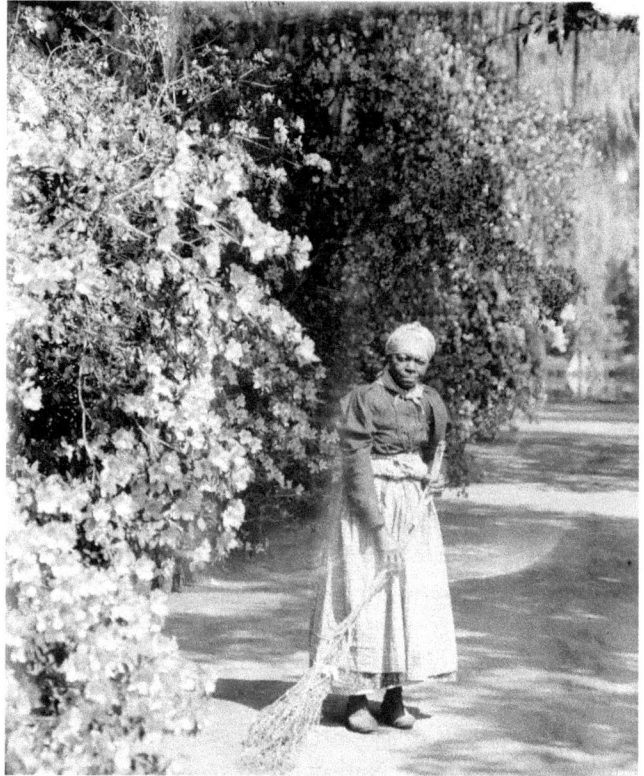

Aunt Phoebe, Magnolia on the Ashley, William Henry Jackson, photographer. *Courtesy Library of Congress.*

Rebecca Campbell, Esther Chandler and Catherine Braxton, who carries the name of her ancestor.

Caesar Bowens had numerous children. One of his children, Richmond Herschel Bowens, was born at Drayton Hall in 1908 and spent his youth there, attentively listening to the stories of his ancestors and respecting their traditional ways of life and values. As a youth, he loved to tend the gardens at Drayton Hall and later worked for Charles Henry Drayton Jr. at 9 Church Street before he went to Chicago at the beginning of World War II. When Bowens returned in the late 1970s, he approached Charles Drayton's son, Charlie, his childhood friend, and explained that he wanted to return to Drayton Hall and be buried there. Drayton introduced Bowens to the National Trust, and the administrators hired him as gatekeeper.

Drayton Hall soon realized that Bowens had more to offer than his role as gatekeeper would allow. He became an interpreter, sharing stories from his youth with visitors on the porch of the Museum Shop and helping to

Charles Henry Drayton III, pictured with Richmond Bowens, who was born at Drayton Hall in 1908. According to Richmond's family history, his ancestors came from Barbados with the Drayton family in the 1670s, and they remained at Drayton Hall after emancipation. Both Charles and Richmond have been devoted to the preservation of Drayton Hall's history. *Courtesy Drayton Hall.*

bring to life the African American history of Drayton Hall. Much beloved, Bowens died in 1998 and is interred in the "Sacred Place." His widow, Velm, asked both Charlie Drayton and George McDaniel, Drayton Hall's executive director, to speak at his funeral. His oral histories and devotion to his family heritage continue to inform and inspire the educational programs of Drayton Hall.

RHETT BUTLER AND THE BLOCKADE RUNNERS

FACT V. FICTION

Margaret Mitchell's Civil War novel *Gone with the Wind* was an immediate sensation. It took Mitchell more than seven years to write, and it was well worth the effort. *Gone with the Wind* sold a record 176,000 copies in the first three weeks of publication in 1936; it has since sold more than 30 million copies. Mitchell won the Pulitzer Prize in 1937. The bestseller was almost immediately adapted into a movie starring Clark Gable and Vivien Leigh. The 1939 film version of *Gone with the Wind* received ten Academy Awards and became the highest-grossing film ever produced in Hollywood up to that time. No sequel or adaptation has enjoyed similar success.

Although Mitchell said that her book was a work of fiction, she drew heavily on her family's war experiences and wove them into the fabric of her book. Part of the close-knit Southern elite, Mitchell's family had long-standing connections with Charleston shipping magnate, George Alfred Trenholm.

Trenholm had been a troubleshooter for the Confederacy's Quartermaster Corps, and Mitchell's grandfather, John Stephens, spent much of the war serving in the Quartermaster Corps in Atlanta. Stephens's wife, Annie, lived with the Mitchell family at the end of her life. Like most Southern ladies of her generation, Annie Stephens would have been a repository of stories about the tragic war and its horrible consequences. It was well known that Trenholm ran a big part of his business from his 172 Rutledge Avenue home, and Margaret Mitchell's aunts had lived there with the sisters of Our Lady of Mercy for a short period after the war. In addition, Margaret Mitchell's brother, Stephens, had written about Trenholm's connections to the Atlanta Rolling Mill and Atlanta Armory and made her promise to use that material in her work.

Thanks to Hollywood, Scarlett O'Hara, the manipulative Southern belle who loses her man in the end, and world-wise Rhett Butler, who learns that money can't buy everything, have become part of the American psyche. Ignorant of Trenholm's financial genius or the role he played in the Confederate war effort, some now claim that Mitchell used Trenholm as the prototype for Rhett Butler.

Butler is an unlikely hero. Introduced as a Charlestonian with a "most terrible reputation," he was born to a patrician family, expelled from West Point for drunkenness and disowned for his scandalous behavior. Worse, the charming scoundrel soon becomes a wildly successful blockade runner who profits shamelessly from his countrymen's privations.[56]

Clark Gable's performance gave Rhett Butler an allure that is timeless. People *want* to believe that he really lived. In contemporary Charleston, tour guides may point out mansions that were once associated with the "real Rhett Butler," claiming that he was none other than the Confederate blockade runner George Alfred Trenholm; they may describe a few similarities between the two men. And that is where fiction and reality part company.

GEORGE ALFRED TRENHOLM: SELF-MADE MILLIONAIRE

George Alfred Trenholm (1807–1876) figured prominently in Charleston's history. His contemporary, Reverend Dr. A. Toomer Porter,[57] painted a vivid picture:

> In business Mr. Trenholm was king. He was the absolute master of local banking and the cotton trade. He had his ships, and his word in Broad Street and on East Bay was law; but it is of the man I would write. He was tall and handsome, graceful in his manners…he had the sweetest smile of any man I ever saw…His alms were not so well known…but I, his pastor, saw what he would not let the world see, and many families that the community knew not of, were made comfortable and lived in ease because of his generosity. He had the clearest mind I ever met with; there was scarcely a subject you could propose that he would not throw light upon. He was the

George Alfred Trenholm. *Courtesy Ethel Nepveux.*

least resentful man I ever knew; of those who did him much harm, he never said a harsh word; of his family circle he was the very light. Great as he was in business, he seemed to leave all at the gate when he came home, and was as tender to his dear wife (who was a perfect Christian woman) as if he were a young lover, and to his children, climbing on his shoulders, and hanging round his neck, he was devoted.

...He succeeded Mr. C.G. Menninger as Secretary of the Treasury of the Confederate States. He, along with Mr. Wagner, inaugurated the blockade-running. They brought immense stores, and guns, and ammunition into the Confederacy. It is a sad commentary that the generation of to-day, even in this community [Charleston], have little knowledge of the greatest man who ever lived in it.[58]

Trenholm's grandfather, William Trenholm, had been a Loyalist who had immigrated to Holland during the Revolutionary War. The family returned to Charleston in 1787 after a brief sojourn in Santo Domingo. According to

The dock. *Courtesy Charleston Museum, Charleston, South Carolina.*

family tradition, William's son was a sea captain who returned to the island to marry the daughter of the Comte de Greffin, a French landowner. Upon discovering that she had already married, he wed her sister, Irene, instead. The couple had seven children and lived in New York for a while. With his father's death, young George Trenholm's education stopped at sixteen. He went to work for John Fraser and Company, one of Charleston's leading Sea Island cotton exporters.[59]

The offices of John Fraser and Company were located at the North Central Wharf at the foot of Cumberland Street. The wharf had immense warehouses and long rows of offices that handled its far-flung international trade. At its peak, John Fraser and Company could handle twenty thousand bales of cotton in a morning. By 1854, the firm commissioned two 767-ton ships to be built in Bath, Maine, specifically designed for the Charleston-Liverpool trade. In addition, it purchased more ships and part interest in others. In 1860, John Fraser and Company advertised an exclusive line of monthly Charleston-Liverpool sailing packets: *Susan G. Owens, Eliza Bonsall, Gondar, Emily St. Pierre* and the *John Fraser*, named in honor of the company's founder.

By the early 1850s, George A. Trenholm had become the senior partner and principal owner of John Fraser and Company, with copartners John Fraser, Edward L. Trenholm, Theodore Wagner, James T. Welsman and Charles K.

Prioleau. The firm had interlocking directorates with Trenholm Brothers in New York City and Fraser, Trenholm and Company in Liverpool, England.

Within a very short period of time, George Trenholm also had major interests in banking circles and was part owner and president of the Bank of Charleston, on whose board of directors he served for forty years.

In 1839, Trenholm purchased a plantation called Springfield in St. Andrew's Parish from Henry Toomer, a relative of his wife through marriage. Her brother, Francis Simmons Holmes, had married Elizabeth S. Toomer, and the couple had moved to Springfield to use it as an experimental farm. Holmes engaged in a wide variety of agricultural management programs and in 1842 published *The Southern Farmer and Market Gardner*. He was also interested in paleontology and geology. In 1837, he discovered phosphate nodules in an old rice field. In 1842, during his agricultural and geological survey of South Carolina, Edmund Ruffin declared the phosphate useless as fertilizer. Years later, when Ruffin's prediction was proven wrong, Holmes claimed credit for the discovery.

Trenholm became involved in politics and espoused the states' rights policies of John C. Calhoun. In 1830, he began to write under the pseudonym "Mercator," penning numerous articles supporting the construction of a railroad between Louisville, Cincinnati and Charleston. He served on the board of the Blue Ridge Railroad before and after the war.[60] By 1842, he had become associated with Robert Barnwell Rhett, the *Charleston Mercury* "fire-eater." He was elected to the South Carolina House of Representatives in 1852 but later resigned because of an unintended conflict of interest. He also represented Charleston three other times in the 1850s and 1860s. In the secession fever of 1860, he was again serving in the state House. He was elected one of the commissioners for the defense of the state and was on the committee to build ironclad steamboats that were financed by Charleston merchants.

Once hostilities started, Trenholm Brothers, located at 42 Pine Street in heart of New York's financial district, closed its office. Branch offices were set up in Nassau and Bermuda under other names, and the company's ships were immediately involved in the war effort. Historian Edward Boykin called Fraser, Trenholm and Company the South's "alter ego," the "omnipresent fiduciary agents" and "member in absentia of the Southern cabinet."[61]

Located in Liverpool, Fraser, Trenholm and Company became a depository for Confederate funds. It acted as the financial clearing house for Confederate agents who supervised the blockade running. The firm ran a fleet of blockade runners that, in return for cotton, turpentine and tobacco, supplied the Confederate government with armaments and needed provisions.

MARITIME ACTIVITIES

According to Trenholm's biographer, Trenholm firms either owned outright or had interest in 120 merchant ships. They purchased three two-thousand-ton steamers, *Bermuda*, *Victoria* and *Adelaide*, and soon other transatlantic vessels joined the fleet. Ownership of many vessels was transferred to British registry to maintain the illusion that they were noncombatant merchant ships. In spite of the ruse, some merchant ships were captured as prizes of war, while others were sunk by the increasingly oppressive Union blockade.

For example, the side-wheel steamer *Ruby*, controlled by Fraser, Trenholm and Company, made eight successful runs through the blockade and had been turned back only once before she ran aground on the Folly Island breakers on her tenth voyage. Captain Peat ordered most of the cargo

Beached remains of the British-built blockade runner *Ruby*, run aground after passing the Federal squadron, June 10–11, 1863, Folly Beach. *Courtesy Library of Congress.*

thrown overboard in an unsuccessful attempt to free the ship. Before she was abandoned, the *Ruby* was set on fire. The crew waded ashore in neck-deep water, while Federal forces fired at them with grapeshot and canister. Union soldiers from Morris Island scavenged the wreckage later.[62]

John Fraser and Company bought some of the first merchant ships seized by privateers, retrofitted them as blockade runners and sent them on their way. Under the command of Captain Thomas Lockwood, the *Gordon* was the first blockade runner to become famous; in fact, she was so successful that the Union called her the "Black Witch."

Before the war, Lockwood had worked for the Florida Steam Packet Company, an ancillary of John Fraser and Company. He eventually became captain of the *Carolina*, a sidewheel packet that transported passengers, mail and cargo between Charleston and Jacksonville. In July 1861, he received a commission as a Confederate privateer and was given command of the *Theodora*, sister ship to the *Carolina* (*Kate*), which had been armed with deck guns. Lockwood started his blockade-running career when he broke through the blockade and captured the *William McGilvery*. He went on to take Confederate commissioners James M. Mason and John Slidell through the blockade to Cuba, where Captain Charles Wilkes, commanding the USS *San Jacinto*, took the two men off the *Trent*, a British mail packet, causing a diplomatic incident that almost brought England to war against the North.

Lockwood's blockade-running exploits and arrant boldness soon earned him celebrity status. When he was in Nassau, the fully loaded *Gladiator* arrived from England, and the British captain did not want to risk facing Union ships waiting outside the harbor. The Trenholm firms soon obtained permission to "break bulk" and transport the cargo piecemeal in other, smaller, faster ships. The *Kate* and another ship were loaded with the *Gladiator*'s cargo. Always flamboyant, Lockwood widely proclaimed that he would take the ship to Halifax and then ran the cargo into the unguarded port of Mosquito Inlet, Florida. Lockwood's runs were so frequent and successful that his exploits became legendary. The *New York Times* commented: "Let us console ourselves like Mr. Disraeli, by allowing [Lockwood's activities] to increase our respect for the energy of human nature." Thomas Lockwood remained a blockade runner with the firm until the war ended.[63]

The Confederate War Department deposited its funds with Fraser, Trenholm and Company, which in turn organized the building of Confederate warships. Because England was supposed to be a neutral country, the vessels were commissioned to be built under the names of fictitious buyers or noncombatants. Once they left the shipyards and were beyond English territorial waters, the ships were outfitted for war and assigned Confederate officers and crews. The Fraser, Trenholm and Company manager in Liverpool, Charles Prioleau, helped supervise the construction of the *Alabama* and kept the plans in his office. He bought the furnishings, financed the ships that took the armaments out to sea and paid the *Alabama*'s expenses the entire time the cruiser was in service.

The most famous warships that Fraser, Trenholm and Company financed were hulls #345 and #290, the most technologically advanced battleships of their time. The first to be completed was #345, supposedly built for an Italian under the name *Oreto*. Once at sea, her name was changed to *Florida*, a ship that became one of the most audacious commerce raiders in the annals of the Confederate navy, with a confirmed thirty-seven prizes, two of which vessels took twenty-three more prizes.

Florida's sister ship, hull #290, was built in great secrecy across the river from Liverpool in Birkenhead, England. The contract was arranged in 1862 by James Dunwitty Bullock through the offices of Fraser, Trenholm and Company.

Bullock's shipbuilding activities in Liverpool had not gone unnoticed by spies, who reported to Thomas Dudley, the U.S. consul. Dudley, in turn, reported the violation of British neutrality to the U.S. ambassador in London. After the *Oreto* was allowed to leave port, Dudley hired an army of spies to keep tabs on hull #290. British customs officials found nothing amiss during construction and let her be outfitted with steam engines and given an English captain and crew.

When Bullock heard that #290, by then the fully outfitted *Enrica*, was about to be seized by British authorities, he hastily invited a group for a festive sea trial. *Enrica* slipped down the Mersey accompanied by the tug *Hercules*. Late in the afternoon, Bullock informed the guests that the *Enrica* needed to be out all night for trials and accompanied his charges back to port on the *Hercules*.

Rid of her guests, the *Enrica* headed out to sea and sailed to the Azores. Captain Raphael Semmes met them at Terceira Island and took command. The vessel was armed and was commissioned *Alabama* on August 24, 1862.[64]

Because U.S. Minister Charles Francis Adams had complained that #290 was bound for the Confederacy, the escape ruse became an embarrassment to the "neutral" British government, which later prohibited the launching of two additional ironclad ships then under construction.

Spanning the globe, *Alabama* never visited a Confederate port. The *Alabama* crew boarded nearly 450 vessels and burned 65 Union vessels, mostly merchant ships. The *Alabama* captured two thousand prisoners without a single loss of life—captured ships' crews and passengers were detained only until they could be placed aboard a neutral ship or put ashore in a friendly port. By June 1864, the *Alabama* had been at sea for 534 days and was headed into port at Cherbourg, France, for badly needed maintenance.

The *Alabama* had eluded the USS *Kearsarge* for almost two years. When Captain Winslow learned of her whereabouts through the Union minister to France, the *Kearsarge* hastened to Cherbourg and lingered offshore with the anticipation of capturing or destroying the rebel warship.

Although his practice had been to hit and run instead of risking destruction by direct confrontation, Captain Semmes notified Captain Winslow through diplomatic channels that he intended to fight. People heard of the impending sea battle, and an estimated fifteen thousand spectators flocked to witness the action, including the captains, families and crews of two merchant vessels that the *Alabama* had destroyed just a few days before entering port.

On June 19, the *Alabama* steamed out, escorted by a French iron-clad frigate whose orders were to ensure that the battle took place outside French territorial waters. In her wake was a small steamer, the *Deerhound*, flying the flag of the Royal Mersey Yacht Club. When they reached international waters, the frigate turned back to Cherbourg. The *Deerhound* continued on behind and stayed near the battle.

The CSS *Alabama*, 1862–64, engraving published in *Harper's Weekly*, 1862. *U.S. Navy photograph.*

Alabama fired first, and the two warships circled and exchanged volleys for almost an hour before the *Alabama* was hit below the waterline. When the *Alabama* struck her colors, the *Kearsarge* ceased firing; however, some renegade junior officers on the *Alabama* decided that they would never surrender and began firing the port guns. After another broadside from the *Kearsarge*, a white flag appeared over the stern. Again Captain Winslow ordered a cease fire; the entire battle lasted one hour and two minutes.

As the *Alabama* was sinking, Captain Semmes sent a boat to the *Kearsarge* to ask for assistance. The wounded and those who could not swim were put into the remaining boats. Just before his ship went down, Captain Semmes threw his sword overboard and jumped into the sea along with his remaining men.

Captain Winslow asked the *Deerhound* to help rescue the men in the water; she took aboard about forty of the *Alabama*'s crew, including nineteen officers, and headed toward England instead of turning them over to the *Kearsarge* as prisoners of war. Much to the distress of his crew, Captain Winslow was forced to watch his prey escape, for he refused to fire on the neutral vessel as it slowly disappeared from view.[65]

THE PRICE OF SOUTHERN PATRIOTISM

Back in Charleston, Trenholm had been an adviser to his close friend, Secretary of the Confederate Treasury C.G. Memminger. When he resigned in July 1864, Trenholm was appointed to fill the vacancy. He withdrew from his business enterprises and moved his family to Richmond. Because of his shipping experience, it was hoped that Trenholm could maintain shipping regulations that were intended to prohibit speculators from importing luxuries when the war effort desperately needed materiel. Trenholm knew that the situation was bad, but he didn't realize the actual conditions until he took office. He tried to float a French loan to reform the inflated currency and recommended heavy taxes to reduce runaway inflation. But the inevitable end was in sight, and in less than a year, military reverses put an end to the Confederate States of America.[66]

The Friday before Richmond fell, Jefferson Davis sent his wife and children, as well as the Trenholm daughters, to Charlotte under the escort of Burton Harrison, President Davis's trusted personal secretary,[67] and Midshipman James Morris Morgan, who had once served on the cruiser *Georgia*. (Early in the war, while he was in Charleston, Morgan had been befriended by George Trenholm; he had fallen in love with Trenholm's daughter, Helen,

A crippled locomotive outside of the Richmond and Petersburg Railroad depot, 1865. *Courtesy Library of Congress.*

whom he later married.) After Mrs. Davis and her children were settled in Charlotte, Morgan and the Trenholm girls proceeded to Abbeville, where Trenholm had secured a house for his fleeing family.

On Evacuation Sunday (April 2), retreating Confederate soldiers set fire to bridges, ships, the armory and warehouses. Amid the chaos, President Davis and his cabinet, minus Secretary of War Breckenridge, traveled on the last train out of Richmond. The poor condition of the roadbed caused the train to make frequent stops. Trenholm was suffering from neuralgia, and his wife, the only woman in the party, tenderly cared for her husband. Her seemingly inexhaustible supply of peach brandy cheered the thirty Confederate officials as they continued on to Danville, the last capital of the Confederacy (April 3 to 10).[68]

General Lee surrendered on April 9, and on April 14, President Lincoln was assassinated. Fearing for their safety, the Confederate officials quickly headed farther south. It was a rough journey. At one point, the party tried to walk on a road so muddy that red clay oozed over their shoe tops. Already sick, the fifty-eight-year-old Trenholm vomited violently from the exertions; he arrived in Charlotte in an ambulance and was immediately put under doctor's care.

The refugees continued to Fort Mill, South Carolina. People along the way clamored for Treasury Secretary Trenholm to rescue their fortunes by redeeming worthless Confederate bonds for gold. While in Fort Mill, Trenholm resigned on April 27 due to ill health. Jefferson Davis proceeded to Washington, Georgia, where the Confederate government was dissolved on May 5. Davis was captured five days later. (Secretary of State Judah P. Benjamin had slipped away before the cabinet reached Washington.)

The Trenholm family reunited in Abbeville and proceeded on to Columbia. Their elegant home had been destroyed by the invading Yankee army, but with $3,000 in gold coins, Trenholm was able to purchase another house from someone who was anxious to leave the city.

The respite was brief. Theodore Wagner was one of the partners at John Fraser and Company. The provost marshal in Charleston threatened to charge him with treason if he did not pay a $10,000 bribe. Not wanting to be executed as a traitor, Wagner paid.

Sensing easy money, army officials decided that the head of the firm and a former member of Jefferson Davis's cabinet would be willing to pay far more. Trenholm was summoned from Columbia to answer charges of treason. He was permitted to travel without a military escort, accompanied by James Morgan.[69]

According to Morgan, they brought a portmanteau full of twenty-dollar gold pieces, which were checked at the station just before they were met by black soldiers. The weary travelers were marched over rough cobblestones and muddy, unpaved streets to the city jail, where the soldiers proceeded to incarcerate Trenholm like a common criminal. When Morgan attempted to follow, he was struck in the stomach with a gun butt with such force that he vomited. He was left outside in the gutter to fend for himself. Morgan found a room eventually and hired a man with a wheelbarrow to haul the heavy luggage to his quarters.

The day after his incarceration, Trenholm was taken in a handsome carriage to meet the greedy military officials. When he refused to pay a bribe for his release, he was unceremoniously marched back to jail under the rough watch of black soldiers.

While this was going on, a concerned Morgan left his rooming house. He ran into an Annapolis classmate who was able to obtain a permit for Morgan to visit the jail. He was horrified to find Trenholm in a filthy cell recently vacated by a convicted murderer; the only furnishing was straw strewn on the floor. The door was left open so that a sentry could monitor the conversation.

In a whisper, Trenholm advised Morgan to take the gold to the daughter of his firm's attorney, James L. Petigru, who had enjoyed a national reputation

Rhett Butler and the Blockade Runners

The District Jail (renovated by Barbot and Seyle, 1855–57). *Courtesy Charleston Museum, Charleston, South Carolina.*

as "the Union man of South Carolina." Petigru had died in 1863, but among his friends was Abraham Lincoln, and the president had instructed the occupying forces to extend every courtesy to Petigru's family.

Susan Petigru King was a beautiful young widow who was well known for her wit and charm; she had already made a name for herself as a novelist of some repute. Trenholm had been supporting Petigru's family after he died, and he knew that she could be trusted.

Morgan presented himself at the King residence. Waiting at the door, he could see Union officers in the parlor. Mrs. King met him and agreed to help. In those lawless times, it was far too dangerous to walk the streets at night carrying a heavy valise, so Morgan returned to his room and stuffed his clothes with coins. When he returned, Mrs. King excused herself from her guests and went upstairs.

While Morgan unloaded his vest pockets, trousers and hip pockets, as well as the breast and tail pockets of his coat, Mrs. King carefully spread the gold between the mattresses of her bed. Morgan was forced to make several trips before he finished delivering his precious hoard. Mrs. King and her manservant kept chuckling during their clandestine activities. Finally, when she could contain herself no longer, she explained the irony of the situation: among her guests downstairs were the provost marshal and the commanding general, whom she had charmed into giving her a permit to visit the unfortunate Trenholm.

The elegant Mrs. King visited Trenholm frequently. She was observed sitting on the filthy straw weeping copiously while the courtly old gentleman tried to comfort her.

Finally, Major John Hatch wrote to his commanding officer and asked what he should do with his prominent prisoner. Hatch was ordered to send Trenholm to Fort Pulaski, Georgia, via Hilton Head, then under the command of General Quincy Gilmore. As they had been friends before the war, Gilmore greeted Trenholm warmly, got his parole and sent him back to Columbia because of his ill health. This infuriated General Sickles, commander of the Department of South Carolina, who wrote to Washington. Gilmore was relieved of his command, and Secretary of War Stanton ordered Trenholm transported to Fort Pulaski to join the other members of Davis's cabinet (excluding Judah Benjamin and General Breckinridge, both of whom had managed to escape to England).

The captive men endured the tedium of a hot, humid Georgia summer and swarms of bloodthirsty mosquitoes. On October 11, 1865, President Andrew Johnson paroled Trenholm and three other prisoners.[70]

PICKING UP THE PIECES

The Trenholm family moved back to their Charleston home at 172 Rutledge Avenue on July 25, 1866. By then, their children were grown and getting married.

In the fall, Dr. Porter visited Trenholm and mentioned that he wanted him to ask President Johnson for a pardon. Although this was required to restore citizenship and property, at that time no Confederate cabinet member had yet applied. The strong-willed Trenholm flatly refused, stating, "I have done nothing of which I am ashamed and have committed no offence for which to ask Mr. Johnson's pardon. I will not do it."

The persistent Dr. Porter did manage to get Trenholm to write a letter elaborating the duty of the Southern people. It was a "masterly production." Porter took it to General Sickles and petitioned an endorsement, stating that men like Alfred Trenholm were essential to the business welfare of the city and the state. Sickles enthusiastically endorsed the letter and returned it, whereupon Porter informed Trenholm that he was heading north.

Number 172 Rutledge Avenue. *Courtesy Charleston Museum, Charleston, South Carolina.*

Dr. Porter carried with him numerous other petitions, including those of Sue Petigru King and her sister, Jane Petigru. The Sisters of Our Lady of Mercy in Charleston wrote, saying, "In our efforts to afford relief to the Union Soldiers confined in the Prisons and Hospitals, we have never applied in vain for aid to the Honorable Gentleman, and we can testify to the liberality and readiness with which he always supported our works of Charity."[71]

Not content with Southern petitions, Dr. Porter traveled to New York City and obtained the signatures of influential Republicans before proceeding on to Washington. The following morning, he arrived at the White House and waited all day for an audience, but to no avail. The next day, through the enticement of numerous cigars, the porter finally admitted him to see the president late in the afternoon. Dr. Porter had met President Johnson before, when he acquired the Marine Hospital for the colored school and reminded him of the occasion. Although Johnson had refused to sign pardons that were purchased, he was happy to put his signature on Trenholm's and charged his own son with expediting it through appropriate channels. It took the godly Dr. Porter just three days to accomplish what others had failed to do in months. The pardon was granted on October 15, 1866.[72]

Once restored to citizenship, Trenholm returned to finance. He reestablished a cotton brokerage under the name of George A. Trenholm and Son.

Before the war, Trenholm's brother-in-law, Francis Simmons Holmes, had already published a second volume on South Carolina fossils. Dr. Holmes and Dr. N.A. Pratt, a distinguished Georgia chemist, continued their study on phosphates after the war. They took their findings to Philadelphia and located financiers to provide startup funds to begin the Charleston Mining and Manufacturing Company. In 1867, the company began mining nearly ten thousand acres of phosphate deposits on both sides of the Ashley River. Holmes was the company's first president, and George Trenholm was on its board of directors. In addition, Trenholm mined phosphate tracts located near Bee's Ferry (Vaucluse, Springfield and Ashley Hall). G.A. Trenholm and Son became the largest phosphate exporter in Charleston. Phosphate mining became vitally important because it helped the community recover from war losses. Even the freed slave laborers benefited because they were not bound to their jobs and could leave at will.[73]

The Greenville and Columbia Railroad went bankrupt in 1871 and was taken over by the South Carolina Railroad. George Trenholm and his son, William, were two of its directors.[74]

Phosphate dock. *Courtesy Charleston Museum, Charleston, South Carolina.*

Trenholm and his partners were involved in numerous lawsuits with the federal government, which claimed that they had illegally converted Confederate dollars into personal assets. The government obtained the books of John Fraser and Company and demanded import duty plus interest on everything that came through the blockade. To pay the taxes, the government sold the company's real estate assets at a fraction of their worth, for property values were severely depressed after the war.[75] The government very aggressively went after the assets of Fraser, Trenholm and Company in Liverpool and ultimately forced it into bankruptcy. In addition, people holding George Trenholm mortgages sued for cash instead of repossessing their properties.

After the war, the United States government sued Great Britain for damages done by warships built in Britain and sold to the Confederacy. Because of the *Alabama*'s amazing interruption of maritime commerce, the suit was known as the Alabama Claims. Once international arbitration endorsed the American position, Britain paid the United States government $15.5 million in 1872. Some have speculated that the British government exchequered a Fraser, Trenholm and Company account and used the money to pay part of the fine.

Trenholm became ill in July 1875; his health continued to decline throughout the following year. In 1874, he was elected to the state House of Representatives, where he was considered one of the few respected white men who could work with the generally detested radical Reconstruction government. He lived just long enough to witness the election of General Wade Hampton as governor and died on December 9, 1876.

Tributes to George A. Trenholm were numerous. As he had been president of the chamber of commerce, after his death flags of almost one hundred ships from many nations flew at half mast in Charleston Harbor.

Litigation from Trenholm's wartime pursuits dogged him until the end of his life and beyond. To settle the indebtedness of his estate, properties of G.A. Trenholm and his deceased partner, James Welsman, were auctioned off in April 1879. This included sale of 172 Rutledge Avenue, where Trenholm's wife, Anna Helen Holmes Trenholm, had lived for thirty-four years.[76]

The lovely Trenholm mansion was purchased by banker Charles Otto Witte. Laura Witte Waring's memories of post-Reconstruction Charleston are recorded in *The Way It Was in Charleston, S.C.: Recollections of a Southern Lady, 1877–1975*. In 1907, Witte's daughters sold 172 Rutledge Avenue to Mary Vardrine McBee, who founded Ashley Hall School for Girls on the property.

Tower of the Winds

The Dilettanti

In the days when a classical education was valued, few educated people in
the English-speaking world did not thrill to the epic stories of ancient Greece
and Rome. The Trojan Horse and Blind Homer were as familiar as Caesar's
Gallic wars and Hannibal crossing the Alps. Throughout the British empire,
students learned both Latin and Greek, and some, no doubt, thought there
was truth in the old doggerel, "I hate Latin, bad as bad can be. First it killed
the Romans and now it's killing me."

Privileged English boys had tutors or were sent to exclusive boarding
schools before attending a university, preferably Oxford or Cambridge.
They learned about the Battle of Marathon, the Spartans at Thermopylae
and the incredible outpouring of philosophy, drama, higher mathematics
and architecture during the Golden Age of Pericles.

Although the educated elite read about the accomplishments of ancient
Greece, there was very little direct contact between the British empire and
contemporary Greece before the mid-eighteenth century. Greece was part
of the Ottoman empire, which made visiting difficult at best, and few Grand
Tours included Athens. As a result, no one had made a comprehensive
study of the Acropolis and other Greek architectural sites, and Roman ruins
remained the classical idiom. Never having seen drawings of the ancient
monuments, it probably never occurred to anyone that Greek buildings
would be different from those in Rome.

It took a group of hedonistic, wealthy and sometimes dissolute English aristocrats to popularize the treasures of the Levant (eastern Mediterranean countries).

It has been said that the rediscovery of Greece begins and ends with the Society of the Dilettanti. The society was formally established in 1732 by two Englishmen who had been on a European Grand Tour. Sir Francis Dashwood was the driving force. He was a libertine whose sexploits were the talk not only of London but also Paris, Rome and St. Petersburg. He and the Earl of Sandwich are alleged to have been members of the notorious Hellfire Club.

By 1743, Horace Walpole had condemned the Society of the Dilettanti's affectations and described it as "a club, for which the nominal qualification is having been in Italy, and the real one, being drunk: the two chiefs are Lord Middlesex and Sir Francis Dashwood, who were seldom sober the whole time they were in Italy."[77]

However, with their wealth and celebrity, Dashwood and Sandwich not only made classical archaeology something of a gentlemen's sport; they made it fashionable and they made it fun! They may have dressed in Roman togas and drank too many toasts, but in spite of the antics, some Dilettanti became important collectors. Others were politicians, national figures, theatrical figures and explorers, and several were among Britain's leading painters.

In 1750, two men were proposed for membership in the society who radically changed the prevailing architectural iconography. They were an unlikely pair.

Nicholas Revette, in his late twenties, was the second son of a Suffolk gentleman. He had been studying painting in Rome and may have been a *cicerone*, or tour guide, for English visitors.

James Stuart, later described as the "Indiana Jones" of his day, was the son of a deceased Scots sailor. He grew up in London with poor prospects. To help support his mother, brother and two sisters, he was apprenticed as a painter to a fan maker at a young age. A talented craftsman, after his mother's death, he was able to set up his siblings in the fan-making business and left England to follow his dreams of studying in Italy.

Traveling to Rome on foot, the impoverished Stuart paid for his expenses by painting fans along the way. In order to read the captions on illustrations, he had already studied Latin while in England; he learned Italian and Greek in Rome and earned a livelihood by painting and serving as a *cicerone* to English visitors. He also gained a reputation as a classical scholar by publishing several essays. His greatest asset, however, was the ability to entice wealthy and influential people to support his enterprises.

Tower of the Winds

Stuart met Revette in Rome. In 1748 they accompanied architect Matthew Brettingham Jr. and painter Gavin Hamilton on a trip to Naples to study monuments in *Magna Grecia*, the site of ancient Greek colonies whose ruins had survived about two thousand years. The group came to the conclusion that contemporary architecture should follow the classical Greek designs instead of derivative Roman examples; they decided to seek funding for an expedition to go to Athens to study Greek prototypes. Revette wrote his father full of enthusiasm about the proposed trip.

Brettingham and Hamilton dropped out before Stuart and Revette set out for Venice, where they were able to interest one of the original founders of the Society of the Dilettanti, Sir James Gray, the English Resident Minister. He organized a subscription list and proposed them for membership.

Once funded, the pair set out for Greece. Part of the Turkish Empire, it was known for its murderous brigands, and traveling there was a dangerous undertaking. The English ambassador at Constantinople used his diplomatic connections to arrange for their safe conduct.

Tower of the Winds from *The Antiquities of Athens, Measured and Delineated by James Stuart and Nicholas Revett, Painters and Architects, 1762.*

Stuart and Revette arrived in Athens in April 1751.[78] Their project progressed slowly. Stuart contributed the topographical views and text, while Revette made measured drawings. They were so meticulous that, on one occasion, they arranged for the house surrounding the Tower of the Winds be torn down in order to make accurate measurements.

The attention to detail caused the suspicious Turks to regard the group as spies. The pair finally left Athens during disturbances following the death of Osman, chief of the Black Eunuchs. Stuart had other ventures and departed in 1753, only to face hazards in Salonica. Revette fled the following year and was waylaid by Maltese pirates en route to his rendezvous with Stuart in Thessalonica.[79]

Revette remained in Greece, while Stuart returned to England in 1762 and published Volume I of *The Antiquities of Athens and Other Monuments of Greece*. It contained only minor monuments: the temple at Pola and temple of Augustus, the temple on the Ilissus, the Lysicrates monument, the Tower of the Winds and the Stoa. The exquisitely detailed measured drawings were an immediate sensation.

After the publication of Volume I, Stuart bought out Revette's interest. Volumes II–IV of the *Antiquities of Athens* were published posthumously.[80]

Stuart was commissioned by the British statesman and patron of the arts Lord Lyttelton to produce the first Greek building in England. He later designed houses and picturesque teahouses using the celebrated folio drawings. Strict adherence to classic Greek motifs earned him the nickname "Athenian" Stuart. Although financially successful, Stuart led a rather dissipated life and ended up playing skittles in the afternoon and visiting public houses in the evening. After his death, his executor died of madness in a London workhouse, and most of Stuart's valuable papers disappeared.[81]

ATHENS COMES TO CHARLESTON

American colonials copied everything English. Thanks to James Gibbs's design books and those of others, elements of Palladian architecture, based on the Venetian architect Andrea Palladio's interpretation of Greek and Roman prototypes, appeared very early both in public buildings and freestanding private homes along the eastern seaboard of North America.

The early Carolinians certainly liked elegance. In 1723, they built Second St. Philip's Church, a structure that was remarkably similar to what was *au courant* in London. It had a steeple placed within the actual building and three freestanding porticos supported by colossal columns. Recognized as the most architecturally significant building in Charleston, it was thoroughly documented before it burned down in 1835.[82]

After the War of 1812, Lowcountry planters and merchants began to enjoy unimaginable wealth. With their newfound affluence, Charleston City Fathers devised a grand scheme for a gathering place for their elite. When the financial panic of 1837 caused the city to modify their design, they raised money by selling a portion of the proposed park, the strip of land overlooking the harbor. It was there that some of Charleston's

Burning of St. Philip's Church, by John Blake White, 1835. *Courtesy College of Charleston Special Collections Waddell Collection, Charleston, South Carolina.*

most glorious mansions were built. Among the first was Robert William Roper's mansion, built in 1838. Its two-story piazza (Charlestonese for porch) with colossal Ionic columns was intended to dominate the skyline as ships approached from the sea. The imposing Roper house set the standard for its neighbors.

In April 1839, illustrations of the fashionable pure Greek style became readily available when a newspaper advertisement introduced Stuart and Revette to Charleston:

> THE ANTIQUITIES OF ATHENS.
> And other monuments of Greece; as measured
> and delineated by James Stuart, F.R.S., and Nicho-
> las Revett, painters and Architects, illustrated with
> seventy plates, London Edition.
> Just received and for sale by
> W.H. BERRETT, No. 36 Broad-st.
> Ap 3 (near Church.)[83]

It wasn't long before the Tower of the Winds motif began to appear on public buildings and private residences throughout the city.

In 1845, William Ravenel built a house next door to Robert Roper. It, too, had colossal columns supporting a two-story porch, but this one was constructed with massive sandstone fluted columns capped with Tower of the Winds capitals. The impressive Ravenel portico survived Union bombardment but not the earthquake of 1886. Remains of the capitals have been preserved on the property and clearly demonstrate that they were the grandest Tower of the Wind columns built in Charleston.

About 1850, Edward Leonard Trenholm built a mansion at 93 Rutledge Avenue. Again the fashionable Tower of the Winds capitals were used, but this time rendered both in carved wood and cast iron.[84]

Edward Leonard Trenholm was part of the Trenholm shipping empire. On April 7, 1836, he married Eliza Bonsall Holmes, sister of his brother's wife. As part of Fraser, Trenholm and Company, Edward Trenholm lived

Number 93 Rutledge Avenue. *Courtesy College of Charleston Special Collections Waddell Collection, Charleston, South Carolina.*

in Liverpool part time. When Fraser died in 1854, Edward Trenholm left the company.

In 1853, Edward Trenholm purchased Mountain Lodge, a four-hundred-acre estate in Flat Rock, North Carolina. Flat Rock was a small mountain community that had long been a retreat for Charlestonians who wished to escape malaria and the oppressive Lowcountry summers.[85]

Mountain Lodge had been built by Charles Baring for his English-born wife, heiress of a lifetime fortune from her fifth husband, James Heyward of Charleston. After Susan Baring's death, the Heyward wealth reverted to his heirs. Baring needed money and sold Mountain Lodge to Edward Trenholm.[86] He also sold a two-hundred-acre property called Solitude to his brother, George A. Trenholm. The following year, George Trenholm sold Solitude to Henrietta Aiken, wife of the governor.

During the war, some Arkansas troops visited Flat Rock and became quite unruly once they discovered whiskey. According to a letter dated April 2, 1864, from Harriott Middleton to her sister:

> *They went to Mr. [Edward] Trenholm's about dark. A tipsy party of them. Some were posted at his gates, others went to the stable, and three swaggered about the house and ended by collaring Mr. Trenholm, and presenting three pistols at his head. His wife threw herself between them, and the men declared that they could not injure a woman. Mr. Trenholm jumped out of the window and made for the mountain top. They were just going off with three horses when the son, young Savage Trenholm, returned. He was on his way to Greenville when the soldiers stealing his blanket and his servant's blanket insisted on his returning here. He found the household in confusion, his father had disappeared, and they feared had been carried off. So he rushed over to a neighbor for assistance. When they returned together, Mr. Trenholm was seen coming down the mountain. Their horses they will probably never see again.[87]*

The Edward Trenholm property at 93 Rutledge Avenue has passed through many hands. The carriage house was later converted into a private residence (42 Montague Street). The main house has been occupied by a variety of people. According to local tradition, for many years it was owned by an eye doctor. The Junior League rented it as its headquarters, and in 1980 a screenwriter from Los Angeles purchased the property with the intention of retiring in Charleston. He engaged the services of a local architect and divided the house into apartments, keeping the luxury suite on the first floor

The 93 Rutledge Avenue staircase. *Photograph by Richard Donohoe.*

for himself. When his plans did not materialize, he sold the property to Fred and Jane MaDan in 1989.

The MaDans were only three months into a massive renovation project when Hugo devastated Charleston. The hurricane-force winds were so fierce that the colossal piazza columns shuddered in the gusts that hit the south side of the house; 60 percent of the slate roof blew off. After recovering from the storm, the MaDans renovated the house, retaining the luxury quarters for their personal use. They added nineteenth-century wrought-iron gates and created a charming courtyard with a fountain in the center. With trees surrounding the property, city noises are muffled, and visitors can enjoy the sound of the fountain's gently dripping water.

CHARLESTON'S RAILROAD
TYCOONS

G enerations of South Carolinians loved to hate the state's last
 Reconstruction governor, enigmatic Daniel Henry Chamberlain.
Born in West Brookfield, Massachusetts, he graduated with honors from
Yale University in 1835 and attended Harvard Law School. In 1863, he
joined the Union army and served as a second lieutenant with the Fifth
Massachusetts Cavalry, a regiment of black troops. In 1866, he arrived in
South Carolina to settle the estate of a friend. He remained and became a
cotton planter.[88] He also entered Reconstruction politics.

After serving as a member of the South Carolina Constitutional
Convention, Chamberlain was elected attorney general in 1868. He was
involved with railroads as well, for as early as 1870 he wrote about some
railroad manipulations in which he was involved: "There is a stint on money
in this or I am a fool."[89] Chamberlain practiced law in Charleston after
he failed to win the Republican nomination for governor in 1872. He was
elected to the University of South Carolina Board of Trustees in 1873, when
the first black students and faculty joined the institution. He went on to be
elected governor in 1874.

The state was already bankrupt when Chamberlain took office. Dishonest
use of public money and patronage were rampant. One of the very first
acts of the Reconstruction state legislature had been the ordering of several
thousand dollars worth of gold spittoons. Profligate spending had depleted
the state treasury to the extent that there was no money left to cover routine
operating expenses—eventually, even the gas lighting at the state capitol had
been shut off due to delinquent payments.

Chamberlain's campaign for reforms gave white southerners hope that, at last, the corrupt Republican Party could be reformed. In spite of much opposition within his own party, the new governor took action against dishonest and inefficient officials. He allied himself with Reform carpetbaggers in Columbia and white Democrats who hoped for change. With a coalition of cross-party supporters, his chances for reelection in 1876 seemed good.

However, in early 1875, two things changed the political landscape. First, Chamberlain blocked the seating of two Republicans to the bench, the notorious robber governor Franklin J. (Judas) Moses Jr. and W.J. Whipper, calling their election by the legislature "a horrible disaster." He depicted Moses "as infamous a character as ever in any age disgraced and prostituted public position." At the Republican convention, he beat down the most radical Reconstructionists and made an emotional appeal that lasted ninety minutes, chastising his enemies with "a venom-dripping tongue lashing." Mesmerized, the state convention vindicated Chamberlain and elected him as the delegate to the national convention.[90]

Chamberlain's handling of the Hamburg riot in July 1876, though, was a disaster. He called the six deaths a "massacre" and requested that President Grant preserve military order by sending in more troops. This action so disgusted his Democratic allies that they nominated a Straitout ticket headed by the popular ex-Confederate general Wade Hampton III. As one historian commented:

> [T]*he return to Straightoutism was a return by the native whites to their true selves...When South Carolina found Wade Hampton in 1876, it was as if she had re-found herself. Indeed, Hampton was, above all, the creature of the society that had reared him. He was the personification of its ideal, carrying in his human form the inflexible rectitude, the sober courage which all South Carolinians idolized but few possessed.*[91]

Hampton's candidacy opened the doors for the most volatile election in South Carolina history. Tired of occupying soldiers and an administration riddled with greed, the white populace was united under Hampton with a surge of unity never seen before or since in South Carolina.

There was no voter registration, and fraud was perpetrated by both sides. In Charleston, white Democrats escorted black Democrats to the polls through mobs of club-wielding blacks, who shrieked "Kill um! Kill um!" In some counties, there were more votes than there were voters in the 1875 census. Both candidates claimed victory, and the election hinged on disputed votes from Edgefield and Laurens Counties.

While the election results were being contested, President Grant declared South Carolina to be in a state of rebellion. On November 26, he ordered military and naval forces to support the Republican government. In Columbia that evening, in the dark of night, a company of infantry was posted inside the statehouse.

By chance, a group of reporters discovered the troops and quickly telegraphed the "scoop" across the nation. Nothing like this had ever occurred before, and numerous newspaper editorials in other parts of the country expressed outrage that federal soldiers would oversee an election in the United States. On November 27, Governor Chamberlain's deputy ordered the soldiers to refuse entry to the Democratic legislators from Edgefield and Laurens Counties.

Hundreds of men had come to Columbia to witness the opening session of the legislature on November 28. When news that soldiers were occupying the capitol building and that certain Democrats were denied entry reached nearby communities, more of Hampton's supporters hastened into town. By noon, more than five thousand armed and angry men had converged on the capitol grounds, just waiting for the word to attack.

Governor Chamberlain and the army were outnumbered and powerless to prevent bloodshed. Only the restrained intervention of Wade Hampton saved the day. Once order was restored, the House Democrats convened at Carolina Hall and elected General W.H. Wallace as their Speaker.

At the statehouse, E.W.M. Mackey was elected the Republican Speaker in an assembly later to be known as the "Mackey House."

On Thursday, November 30 (Thanksgiving), the Democratic legislators decided to "storm" the statehouse. Walking down several streets in twos and threes so as not to attract attention, they joined forces at the capitol and walked *en masse* through the entrance doors, gaining entrance without incident. General Wallace marched straight to the Speaker's desk and took the chair. When Speaker Mackey heard the news, he angrily rushed into the chamber and attempted to have the Democrats evicted.

Thus began one of the strangest episodes in legislative history. On each side of the House chamber, two legislative bodies with two duly elected Speakers simultaneously went through the motions of conducting business. Afraid of losing their advantage, both parties remained in the Assembly chamber day and night on Thursday, Friday and Saturday. Pistols and rifles were smuggled in. Armed soldiers continued to be posted in the building.

Impatient for Hampton to be sworn in, men began to drift back into the city. It was a volatile situation that couldn't sustain itself for long. On the surface, however, all was calm, and on Sunday night in the statehouse, legislators and reporters bedded down about eleven o'clock.

Nobody knows for sure who warned Wade Hampton late Sunday afternoon of Speaker Mackey's plot to forcibly evict the Democrats from the House chamber with the aid of the unruly Hunkidories who had been hastily summoned from Charleston. Upon investigation, about one hundred fully armed Hunkidories, duly sworn in as deputy sergeants-at-arms, were found concealed in the committee rooms awaiting orders. Democrats inside the House chamber were outnumbered almost three to one, and the confrontation promised to be a bloodbath. It was later speculated that Governor Chamberlain might not have wanted a shootout in the House on his conscience—or in the national news. His authorized biography was strangely silent on this subject.[92]

In his last months spent in office, Governor Chamberlain was described as a "helpless, pathetic figurehead of a disgraced and disappearing party. He rode from house to office and back in a vehicle which looked like half a hearse, a square, windowless carriage, front and side curtains drawn closely so that none could see whether or not he was inside. At office and home he was guarded by soldiers and few were allowed to see him."[93]

The gubernatorial standoff ended in April 1877 when President Rutherford B. Hays withdrew Union troops, and the carpetbagger government collapsed. Chamberlain left the state, and South Carolina thought that it had seen the last of him.

Chamberlain moved to New York City and enjoyed great success as a Wall Street attorney. He was made nonresident professor of constitutional law at Cornell University from 1883 to 1897. Chamberlain also became a friend of Charles Parsons, a New York financier.[94]

The Parsons men were extremely good businessmen. Some of their wealth had come from reorganizing railroads. Charles Parsons had a prestigious position on the New York Stock Exchange, and it was only natural that the struggling South Carolina Railway captured his attention. Charles Parsons was president of the firm that provided $4 million to form the South Carolina and Georgia Railroad Company. He remained in that capacity until he retired in 1899.[95]

The railroad had impressive beginnings, for it was the first company to use steam engines, the first to use an American-made locomotive and the first to carry the state's mail. Its first president was William Aiken Sr., a man who played a major role in the railroad's development.

Charleston's Railroad Tycoons

Aiken was born in 1779 in Antrim, Ireland. He moved to Charleston ten years later and was educated by Mr. Blakley, a cotton merchant. He married Henrietta Watt and fathered two children, William Aiken Jr. (later governor) and Peter. The family moved to 456 King Street in 1807, and it was from there that Aiken assembled the men and money to execute the incorporation of the rail line.

Chartered to expand trade between Charleston and the west, the South Carolina Canal and Railroad was opened in 1833. Unfortunately, Aiken never lived to see his efforts come to fruition. In 1831, while inspecting the tracks, he was killed when his horse was spooked by a train's noise and bolted, overturning his gig.[96]

The 136-mile railroad prospered, and in 1843 it merged with the Louisville, Cincinnati and Charleston Railroad Company to become the South Carolina Railroad. The company's assets were almost completely destroyed by the war, and it went bankrupt in 1878. In 1881, it was reorganized as the South Carolina Railway. Continued financial problems, change of road gauge and the destruction by the earthquake of 1886 forced to company into receivership in 1889. The company was reorganized as the South Carolina and Georgia Railroad under the management of South Carolina's ex-governor, Daniel H. Chamberlain.

According to a May 1894 Charleston paper:

> It is often remarked that nothing is more characteristic of this city than her attachment to her old and peculiar institutions. This remark is not more true of anything than of the South Carolina Railroad, called with affection and a touch of sarcasm the "old Reliable." The history of this road is an essential part of the history of Charleston and the State. The oldest railroad of its length in the United States, it is associated with the names of many of our noblest and greatest men. Its financial career was for thirty years after its completion, one of prosperity and pecuniary success. The benefits it conferred, the share it contributed to our common progress was remarkable. The war came and left it a wreck physically and financially. From this it recovered in great measure by the splendid efforts and services of a few devoted citizens of Charleston...The last receiver, Ex-Governor Chamberlain, has doubtless given us correct information of the plans and views of the new owners...the gentlemen who now own the road are men of independent means, able to own and hold and support the property; that they have bought it for purely business, in distinction from speculative purposes. They have issued no bonds and will issue none to float upon the

markets. The financial hope and interest of the present owners lie in the stock of the road.[97]

By the time Chamberlain returned to South Carolina, public opinion had changed. Disillusioned with Charles Sumner's leadership of radical Reconstruction, Chamberlain authored *Charles Sumner and the Treaty of Washington* and an *Atlantic Monthly* article about Reconstruction entitled "The Frightful Experiment."[98] Reverend A Toomer Porter commented, "I always admired his [Chamberlain's] undoubted ability. I was one of those who gave him every credit for honesty of purpose during the trying days in which he figured in the history of South Carolina."[99] Alfred B. Williams, founder of the *Greenville News*, noted that Chamberlain had become a good friend of South Carolina.[100]

Chamberlain assumed charge of the railroad November 1, 1889, and immediately went to work to increase revenue by adding new lines and increasing rolling stock. To attract local businesses, platforms, sidings and connections were supplied whenever possible.

By 1894, the local newspaper had dubbed Chamberlain a friend of Charleston and quoted him as saying that after twenty-five years of acquaintance with the new owners of the road, "Messers Parsons and their associates are 'experienced business men and practical railroad men' who will make every effort to attract to the port of Charleston a heavy volume of Western business comparable to that now going through Port Royal."[101]

While Chamberlain was busy attempting to stimulate business for the railroad, plans for reorganization were underway. As these attempts were

New shipping facilities. *Courtesy Charleston Museum, Charleston, South Carolina.*

A Charleston dock. *Courtesy Charleston Museum, Charleston, South Carolina.*

unacceptable to the bondholders, the courts ordered that debts be satisfied and the railroad be sold.[102] It was reorganized once again five years later as the South Carolina and Georgia Railroad Company.

In November 1894, the South Carolina General Assembly passed an act confirming the new charter and authorized construction of track through the streets of Charleston to connect with the Cooper River docks. The twenty-three-foot depth of the Charleston bar was particularly attractive to shipping interests.

The railroad purchased about 750 feet of Cooper River waterfront property between Laurens and Society Streets; the acquisition included a 200,000-bushel-capacity elevator and a rice mill to facilitate the shipment of midwestern grain. They added wharves, warehouses, compresses and other terminal structures and extended the track from John Street through Chapel and Washington Streets to terminals on the Cooper River located between Laurens and Society Streets.[103] This was a major transportation upgrade from drayage on mule-drawn wagons.

Merging the South Carolina Railroad into the Southern Railway system to Charleston was heralded as a great event, the realization of a long-ago dream

Bennett's Rice Mill. *Courtesy Harriott Pinckney Means Johnson.*

The rail yard. *Courtesy Charleston Museum, Charleston, South Carolina.*

to connect South Carolina with the west. Southern Railway gained control of the line in 1899 and obtained a lease to it in 1902. The lease is still in effect.

Edwin Parsons became assistant to the president of the Carolina and Georgia Railroad (his father), with an office in New York City. He was also vice-president of the Rome, Watertown and Ogdensburg Railroad and succeeded his father as president until that road was sold. The younger Parsons also served on the boards of other companies until his retirement. He married Mary Battle Whitehead from Savannah in 1899.

Edwin Parsons purchased the remaining four hundred acres of the old Middleton plantation, The Oaks, in Goose Creek. The avenue of stately live oaks planted by Edward Middleton had survived the vicissitudes of time, but the plantation house had not. It had burned down in 1840, and in 1896 Parsons built an eighteen-room mansion designed by the New York architect Walter B. Chambers. Adorned with a colossal white columned half-circle portico, it boasted eight bedrooms, eight bathrooms, a billiard room, a library, two drawing rooms and a living room, as well as servant quarters with dining rooms, a kitchen and a pantry. The house overlooked a small lake bordered by azaleas. Hidden among the azaleas was a playhouse called "The Acorn" where the Parsons children played. It was a pleasant, carefree lifestyle, with plenty of servants. Parsons used it as a winter home, but the Parsons children were educated in New York.

Parsons children at The Oaks. Note that the nurse holding the baby was covered with a rug to prevent her from being in the picture. *Courtesy Harriott Pinckney Means Johnson.*

By the time their youngest child, Mary Battle Parsons, was five, the family started traveling to Europe. In 1908, Captain Smith of the SS *Adriatic* gave the young child a silver loving cup for her fifth birthday. (Smith was later captain of the *Titanic.*)

When Mary Battle Parsons married William Martin Means in 1925, the wedding was celebrated at the historic St. James Goose Creek Church. Edwin Parsons was a vestryman at St. James Goose Creek and member of the executive committee of the Red Cross in Charleston during World War I.

Capturing an alligator at The Oaks. *Courtesy Harriott Pinckney Means Johnson.*

In January 1909, while the Panama Canal was under construction, President Taft visited Charleston to tout the benefits the canal would bring to the local economy. The future looked bright. He and his entourage were wined and dined by local businessmen and politicians. They played golf at the country club, attended religious services at the Unitarian Church and enjoyed visiting Taft's Yale classmate, Edwin Parsons, for a special lunch at The Oaks.

Edwin Parsons died in 1922. His wife sold The Oaks in 1930 and moved to 51 East Bay Street. Built in 1799 by Caspar Christian Schutt, an early German merchant. Following the custom of the day, Schutt located his stores and counting house on the property. The mansion was at one time the residence of John Fraser, senior partner in Fraser, Trenholm and Company.[104] C.T. Lowndes purchased the property in 1830. During the Lowndes ownership, the house next door was demolished to make way for a formal garden. Number 51 East Bay remained in the Lowndes family until it was bought by Mary Parsons one hundred years later.[105]

Once living in town, Mrs. Parsons visited her friends for afternoon teas, transported in a limousine driven by a chauffeur named William. On hot

The Oaks. *Courtesy Charleston Museum, Charleston, South Carolina.*

Number 51 East Bay. *Courtesy Harriott Pinckney Means Johnson.*

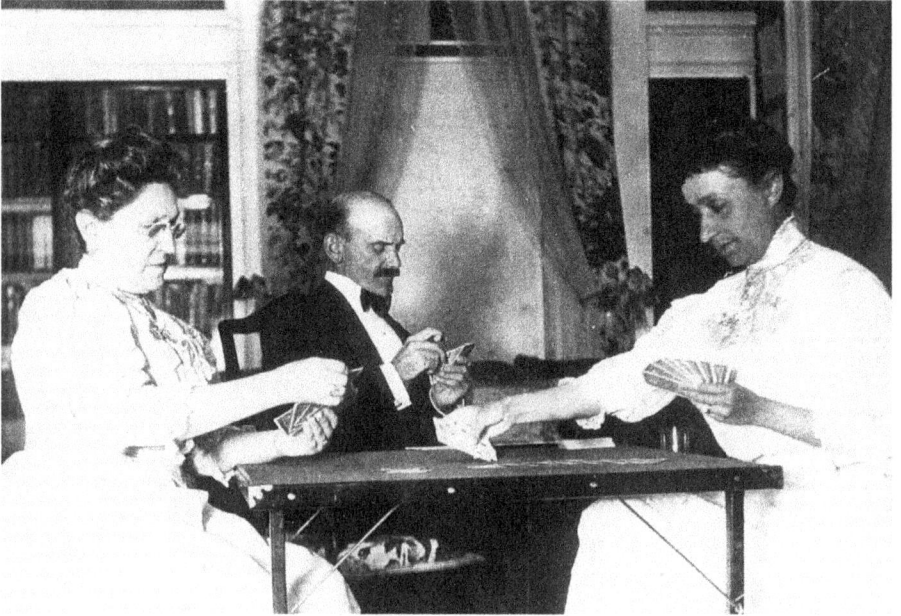

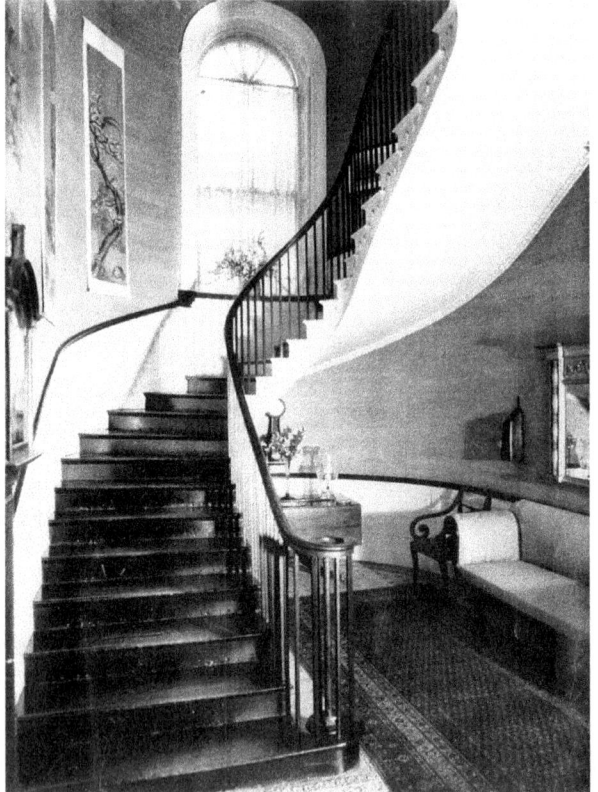

Above: The Parsons family relaxing at The Oaks. *Courtesy Harriott Pinckney Means Johnson.*

Right: The staircase at 51 East Bay. *Courtesy Harriott Pinckney Means Johnson.*

days, she ordered William to take her white terrier Tuppy for a ride around the Battery to cool off. Tuppy would put his front paws on the right front window, lean out and enjoy the breeze.

After Mrs. Parsons died in 1948, 51 East Bay changed hands several times. The present owner has been credited with rescuing the mansion from a planned condominium project. It is still rumored around town that when the condominium was envisioned, the elegant curved staircase was to be removed to make way for an elevator shaft.

As for The Oaks, Charles Sabin, former president of the Guarantee Trust Company of New York, purchased it in 1930; he remodeled the house, removed the stately columns and spent lavishly upgrading the property. In 1956, local businessmen formed The Oaks Company and planned to develop the remaining acreage with a country club, a golf course and exclusive residential homes.[106] In February 2008, the 17,462-square-foot Parsons mansion caught fire in a conflagration that involved seventy firefighters. At the time of the fire, the house was listed for sale at $12 million.[107] There were ugly whispers about the source of the fire.

In 1890, after the death of his wife and four sons, former governor Chamberlain retired to the town where he was born: West Brookfield, Massachusetts. He traveled for a time and later settled in Charlottesville, Virginia, where he died of cancer in 1907.

Descendants of Edwin Parsons continue to live in the Charleston area.

A Modern Wade
Hampton and His Lady

In 1974, South Carolina voters elected Dr. James (Jim) Burrows Edwards as governor in a seismic shift of power that had happened only once before, when the beloved Ex-Confederate general Wade Hampton ousted the corrupt Republican Reconstruction government in 1876. Buoyed up by a strong Christian faith, Governor Edwards and his wife, Ann Darlington Edwards, accomplished more with their modest demeanor than have many more highly visible politicians, and their influence did not stop when the couple left the Governor's Mansion.

Ann's Darlington's father, Stephen, was a Yale-educated mechanical engineer who had worked on both the Lake Murray and the Santee Cooper hydroelectric projects. As the country geared up for war after Pearl Harbor, he was called to Washington, where he contracted with the Defense Electric Power Administration (part of the War Production Board) in the northwest United States. When Stephen Darlington Jr. joined the army, his patriotic younger sister, Ann, wanted to do her part, too. After graduating from high school, she joined the Cadet Nurse Corps. The war ended, however, while she was still in training, so her first assignment turned out to be a polio epidemic in North Carolina.

In the meantime, Jim Edwards, who had grown up in the sleepy village of Mount Pleasant, also wanted to support the nation's war effort. He was too young to enlist, so he tried to join the merchant marine, but he was underweight. Undaunted, the determined young man gorged himself with bananas washed down with milk until he acquired the required poundage. He reapplied, and this time he was accepted. By the time Edwards was able to join, the Allies had gained command of the seaway, and the German submarine threat had been significantly reduced.

While in Europe, the intrepid young sailor just happened to bump into Ann's brother, Stephen Darlington, who was serving with Patton's Third Army. Darlington suggested that he call his sister Ann when he was again stateside. Edwards did just that, and after a long courtship, they married in September 1951.

Twelve days later, the newlyweds moved to Louisville, Kentucky, where Edwards entered the University of Louisville's

"The salty dog," Jim Edwards, the youngest East Coast merchant marine officer in World War II. *Courtesy Dr. and Mrs. James Edwards.*

Dental School. The new bride was hired as the assistant chief nurse at the Louisville Regional Blood Center, an employment that provided an opportunity to interface with a sampling of rural America: the lush Kentucky horse country; the rough, depressed Kentucky mining region; and the bountiful Indiana corn farms. Little did she realize that as she traveled, she was gently being prepared for a far different role in the future. While the Edwardses were in Louisville, son Jim joined the family.

To avoid being drafted after the Korean War broke out, Edwards joined the navy after graduating from Dental School. He was stationed at Chincoteague Naval Air Station, located on an island just off Virginia's eastern shore.

Once his service was completed, the family moved to Philadelphia, where Edwards began graduate study at the Medical University of Pennsylvania. After graduation, Dr. Edwards did his residency in oral and maxillofacial surgery at Henry Ford Hospital in Detroit. Daughter Catharine joined the

A Modern Wade Hampton and His Lady

Ann Edwards's graduation from Columbia Hospital.
Courtesy Dr. and Mrs. James Edwards.

family before they returned to Charleston in 1960. Dr. Edwards began his dental practice, while his wife stayed home, happily raising her two preschool children.

By the time Arizona senator Barry Goldwater ran against Lyndon B. Johnson in 1964, the national Democratic Party was visibly slipping toward socialism. Senator Goldwater championed free enterprise, fiscal responsibility, a strong national defense and small government, ideals that resonated in the Democratic "Solid South." The Edwardses rallied to the call and became heavily involved in local politics. Dr. Edwards served as the Republican county chairman for six years and as the district chairman for two, while his wife helped found the East Cooper Republican Women's group, an organization that became effective on both local and state levels.

In December 1970, the powerful First District congressman L. Mendel Rivers died unexpectedly. When the state held a special election to fill his term, popular wisdom was that Republican Edwards had an even chance of beating the man everyone assumed would be his Democratic opponent: Charleston's popular mayor, Palmer Gaillard. In fact, the Democrats were so confident that while Gaillard was campaigning, his wife had already gone to Washington to look for a house.

It turned out very differently. Having obtained the endorsement of the late congressman's widow, the electorate overwhelmingly supported a young political unknown, Rivers's namesake and godson, Mendel Jackson Davis, who capitalized on the name "Mendel" so heavily that some suspected that sentimental voters actually thought they were resurrecting their beloved congressman. In an astonishing upset, Davis handily won the Democratic nomination and went on to win the special election with a plurality in eight out of nine First District counties.[108] Defeated Jim Edwards thought that his political career was over.

Although Goldwater lost the election, his anticommunist stance had finally made it respectable to be a Republican in the Deep South, the only section of the country that he carried. As antiwar activism and socialistic philosophies continued to splinter the Democratic Party, Dr. Edwards kept looking for candidates who would switch party affiliations. He finally convinced Tommy Hartnett and General Tom Kennedy. Hartnett said that he wouldn't run unless Edwards did. As a result, in 1972 both were elected as senators in the state legislature. During his term, Edwards successfully pushed to have candidates selected by primary elections instead of by party conventions, which cleared the way for him to run in the state's first Republican primary. He won the gubernatorial candidacy in an upset victory.

More sensational that year was the Democratic primary. Seven candidates vied for the state's top political plum. Among them was Charles "Pug" Ravenel, who had returned to South Carolina after an outstanding career up north. A born athlete, he attended the exclusive Phillips Exeter Academy on a football scholarship from the *Post and Courier* and went on to greater glories at Harvard. His Harvard MBA landed him a job with the prestigious investment banker Donaldson, Lufkin and Jenrette in New York. In 1966, he went to Washington on a one-year White House fellowship and became interested in politics.

Flush with success on Wall Street, Ravenel moved back to Charleston in 1972 to start his own investment partnership. He was downtown Charleston's fair-haired boy. In 1974, Ravenel decided to run for governor, reportedly intending to use the office as a steppingstone to the presidency.

Although there was a provision in the state's constitution that required a governor to be a South Carolina resident for five years preceding an election, Ravenel filed and arranged for a friendly suit contesting his candidacy. A state circuit court ruled that he was eligible because he had always intended to return to his home state. With those assurances, Ravenel ran a Madison Avenue campaign unlike anything ever before witnessed in South Carolina. Slick television ads, photo ops and personal charisma wowed the voters, much to the chagrin of the entrenched Democratic hierarchy. Six weeks before the election, Ravenel was leading in the polls by whopping 38 percent. At age thirty-six, he represented the exhilarating "New South." Politically, he was the man to watch.

A disgruntled opponent in the Democratic primary, businessman Milton Dukes, and disc jockey Ben Dekle challenged Ravenel's candidacy, claiming that he failed to meet the state's five-year residency requirement. The South Carolina Supreme Court disqualified Ravenel by a five to zero ruling. With the election rapidly drawing near, the Democratic Party hastily convened a special convention and selected party stalwart William Jennings Bryan Dorn as its substitute candidate.[109]

While Ravenel's ouster was making national news, Dr. Edwards was busily campaigning in the state's media centers. His wife was tasked with making appearances in less populated areas. Already familiar with the rhythm of life in the Lowcountry, she enjoyed meeting the people of the Pee Dee tobacco farms and the bountiful Upstate peach orchards around Spartanburg and Abbeville. She made her speaking début ad-libing on prescribed topics in rural communities.

In spite of the Watergate fallout that elected Jimmy Carter president, Edwards won the South Carolina election with a surprising seventeen thousand vote plurality and made history by becoming the first Republican governor since the hated Reconstruction government was voted out one hundred years before. Victorious Republicans "went wild" celebrating. The Edwardses shook more than five thousand hands on inauguration day, and that was just the beginning.

Making the transition from homemaker to First Lady was challenging. "Jim dragged me to the governor's mansion kicking and screaming," Ann Edwards said later, for she was deeply concerned about how politics would affect their children. The Watergate scandal had rocked the nation, and popular perception was that all politicians were crooks. With support from all over the state, she quickly changed her tune and learned how to use her newly acquired influence effectively.

As the new First Lady had never been in the Governor's Mansion before the election, the outgoing governor's wife, Mrs. West, graciously gave a luncheon in her honor before she herself vacated the premises. Once Mrs. West left, unaware of household protocol, a surprised Mrs. Edwards suddenly found herself alone with inmates from local correctional facilities and their supervising highway patrolman. As she quickly learned, the staff consisted of convicted murderers, who were considered more desirable than habitual thieves and drug users. The inmates were well trained, however, and knew exactly how to function with southern graciousness. This was fortunate, for the new governor's wife was told that she had to start entertaining immediately. In the first six weeks, the Edwardses entertained more than 1,800 people. While the governor received members of the state Supreme Court, state legislators and industrial leaders, the First Lady presided over a series of breakfasts, lunches, teas, dinners and house tours.

Mrs. James Byrnes was among the first to be honored at a luncheon. The late Governor James E. Byrnes had been one of South Carolina's most distinguished and versatile political figures, and Mrs. Byrnes shared her experiences while living in the "Governor's House." When Mrs. Edwards later asked for a copy of a book about the governors who occupied the mansion, she was told that none existed. First Lady Edwards took up the challenge and decided to create one. She enlisted the help of Augustus T. Graydon, who had knowledge of governors going back to Tillman. The project began under the direction of Dr. Walter Edgar from the University of South Carolina's History Department; the late Dr. George Rogers; and George Terry, a doctoral candidate who was assigned to conduct a series of interviews with the former occupants. Accompanied by the First Lady, this outstanding committee of historians interviewed former First Ladies, children of governors and collateral relatives. Jack Leland of the *News and Courier* also contributed.

Money was scarce in 1975, and the state was in an austerity mode. The new governor had promised during the campaign to impose no additional taxes, a promise that he kept. Although he was advised by his administrative assistant not to finance the publication, the governor ignored that recommendation. His confidence was rewarded as brisk sales eventually made a profit. At the request of the superintendent of education, a copy of the book was given to each school in the state.

Early in Governor Edwards's term, the couple attended the National Prayer Breakfast in Washington, D.C., and later went to the South Carolina Prayer Breakfast. Armed with a strong faith in God, Ann decided to initiate a prayer breakfast for the spouses of legislators, Supreme Court justices and coaches. Only one hundred people attended the first breakfast, but within three years, it had become so popular that it was held in the Coliseum to accommodate more than 1,500 attendees.

Due to the severe economic situation in the 1970s, several historically significant pieces of furniture were sold to museums outside of South Carolina. Through her contacts, Ann Edwards established the Governor's Mansion Foundation, which is now the primary income source for acquiring items of historic importance to the state.

Concurrently, with a cooperative legislature, Governor Edwards's administration implemented unprecedented industrial development (the largest in the state's history), established a reserve ("rainy day") fund and created legislation to redistribute education funds for the benefit of poorer school districts. To reduce costs, he also directed each state agency to slash its budget—austerity that left the state in far better condition financially when Governor Edwards's term ended in 1979. Afterward, the family returned to their normal life in Mount Pleasant.

President Carter's popularity had rapidly declined due to his mishandling of the Iranian hostage crisis and poor economic policies. In 1980, charismatic Ronald Reagan easily defeated his opponent, taking all but four states in the nation. The new president appointed Jim Edwards as secretary of energy, and the family moved again—this time to Washington. Hoping to prevent his confirmation, certain Democratic senators were extremely hostile at hearings on Capitol Hill. Howard Metzenbaum, the liberal "Senator No" from Ohio, even sent sixteen staff people to South Carolina to conduct clandestine investigations into Edwards's character.

Once confirmed, at the direction of the president, Secretary Edwards deregulated oil and added significantly to the Strategic Petroleum Reserve. He was successful in reducing the budget of the Department of Energy from $17.0 billion to $10.5 billion. He was the first secretary of energy to address the problem of cleaning up nuclear waste.

Left to right: Barbara Bush, President Ronald Regan, Secretary of Energy Edwards, Ann Edwards and Vice President George W. Bush. *Courtesy Dr. and Mrs. James Edwards.*

Secretary Edwards resigned from the cabinet in 1982 when he was invited to become president of the Medical University of South Carolina (MUSC). Under his leadership, MUSC tripled the size of its campus and became a nationally recognized institution in healthcare, instruction and research. In recognition of his service, the James B. Edwards College of Dental Medicine was dedicated in his honor in February 2010.

Ann Edwards served as the official university. She also served on numerous boards and participated in the Mount Pleasant Sesquicentennial 1987. As member of the Colonial Dames, she was instrumental in helping obtain National Historic Landmark status for the Powder Magazine.

After Hurricane Hugo devastated the Lowcountry, the Edwardses helped with the restoration of Mount Pleasant's Alhambra Hall and St. Luke's Chapel at MUSC. The chapel had originally been a part of the Federal Arsenal complex; it was decommissioned in 1879 and was part of Porter Military Academy campus before MUSC acquired the property. The hurricane winds had almost completely lifted the roof off the chapel. Instead of razing the shell, the Edwardses joined many others and obtained enough funds from the private sector to restore the historic chapel.

Dedication of the James B. Edwards College of Dental Medicine at the Medical University of South Carolina. *Courtesy Dr. and Mrs. James Edwards.*

A Modern Wade Hampton and His Lady

Another preservation challenge occurred when Snee Farm, the 1754 homesite of Founding Father Charles Pinckney, was threatened by urban development. The property was important, for Pinckney had fought in the Revolutionary War and served four terms as governor of South Carolina, as well as serving as a member of both the U.S. Senate and House of Representatives. He was Jefferson's minister to Spain. As one of the principal framers of the Constitution, Pinckney presented so many proposals at the Constitutional Convention in 1787 that he earned the nickname "Constitution Charlie." When George Washington visited South Carolina in May 1791, he enjoyed a breakfast with Governor Pinckney under a huge oak at Snee Farm.

Ann Edwards had just retired from the board of the Historic Charleston Foundation when they asked her and Nancy Hawk to co-chair a statewide effort to save the historic property. Friends of Snee Farm raised enough money to purchase the homesite and the remaining undeveloped twenty-eight acres in 1990. They later gave the property to the National Park Service.

In recognition of her contributions to Mount Pleasant, a street was named Ann Edwards Lane in her honor in 1991. For her seventeen years of service and dedication to the Medical University, she was awarded a doctorate of humane letters in 1996. As she had spearheaded efforts to raise $1 million to endow the first (and only) chair of nursing in South Carolina, it seemed appropriate that MUSC's College of Nursing name that chair after its benefactress.

In retirement, the Edwardses continue to use their sphere of influence wisely.[110]

Jazz and Razzmatazz

The Jazz Age began in the Roaring Twenties, and today many extol jazz as America's only true art form. Unfortunately, the enormous popularity of Mardi Gras and Bourbon Street has enabled New Orleans to eclipse Charleston's rightful recognition as a cradle of jazz.

South Carolinians claim that jazz started in Charleston. The Carolina coast was one of the major places in the Western Hemisphere where Africa met Europe, and the Lowcountry's rich musical heritage dates all the way back to the early days of the colony.

Church music, military music, ribald English bar ballads and contra dances were all enjoyed by the early settlers, who quickly gained a reputation for their love of liquor and song. It did not take the planters long to utilize the talents of their slaves and free men of color, whom they engaged to play music in their homes and at public functions. The enslaved Africans had a predisposition to improvise in all phases of life, and it was only natural that the Gullah people gradually developed their own unique folk music.

Contra dances required musicians to endlessly improvise on a simple tune to keep the music flowing from one song to another. Concerts for Charleston's elite were given at the St. Cecilia Society from 1766 until its musical patronage ended in 1820. Nineteenth-century music followed mainly European tastes, and there were few innovations until students at the Jenkins Orphanage started playing musical improvisations on the streets of Charleston.

In 1891, Reverend Daniel Joseph Jenkins, a black Baptist preacher, founded a private home for African American orphans and waifs. In 1895, the orphanage relocated from King Street to the historic Marine Hospital on Franklin Street. (Robert Mills, best known for the Washington Monument, was its architect.)

In 1866, with the cooperation of the Freedmen's Bureau, the old Marine Hospital became the site of the first southern school for black children. Funding had been obtained by Reverend Dr. A. Toomer Porter, a white Episcopal minister who had gone north with an impassioned plea for help in war-ravaged South Carolina. The school was later closed, and the handsome building was unoccupied when Jenkins acquired it.

The Jenkins Orphanage. *Courtesy Charleston Museum, Charleston, South Carolina.*

Reverend Jenkins's efforts were wildly successful. More than 360 boys were taken in during the first year of operation. Talented young musicians were classically trained and typically performed light classics, overtures and marches. The orphanage soon used its bands for fundraising. Charlestonians and tourists alike loved their music, and the word quickly spread beyond the Holy City. Bands were invited to tour as far north as Canada, south to Florida and west to Wisconsin, as well as the United Kingdom and the Continent. They played in the inaugural parades of Presidents Theodore Roosevelt and William Howard Taft. A band performed at the 1904 St. Louis World's Fair, and in 1914, they were the only entertainment from the United States at the Anglo-American Exposition in London.

Orphanage bands would end their popular impromptu performances with "hot" music, lively melodies and syncopated rhythms, producing a "ragged" sound, a precursor to what we now call jazz. Band members, usually led by the student conductor, swung into West African–rooted dance steps that eventually evolved into the "Charleston," the dance craze of the Jazz Age. Throughout the 1930s, there were sometimes as many as five Jenkins Orphanage bands on tour during the summer months.

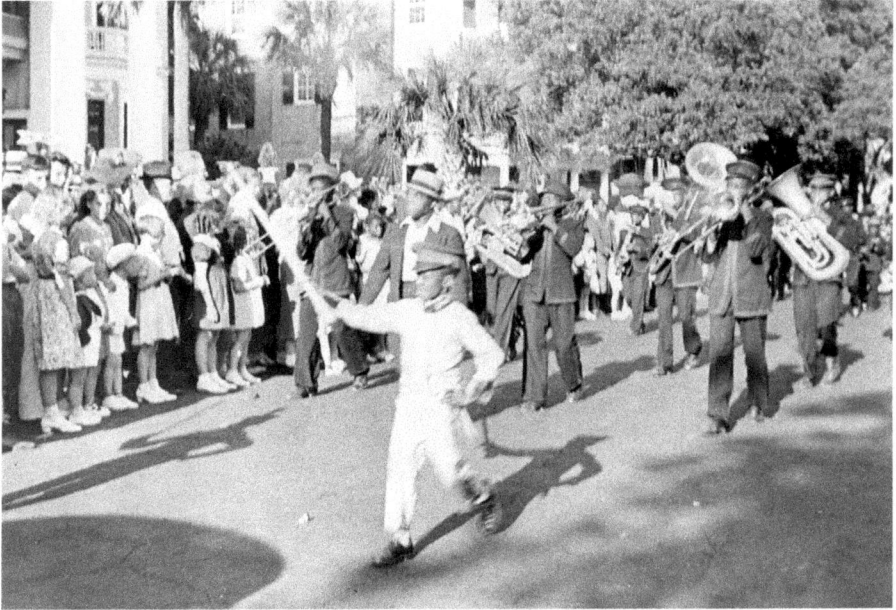

The Jenkins Orphanage marching band. *Courtesy Charleston Museum, Charleston, South Carolina.*

Toward the end of the nineteenth century, African Americans began to migrate to the big cities of the Northeast. In New York, James P. Johnson, a black pianist and composer, played an important role in promoting Charleston after observing the musical beat of southern dockworkers. Having studied both classical and "ragtime" music, Johnson started playing professionally in a sporting house. He progressed to rent parties, bars and vaudeville. He watched the transplanted African Americans entertain and dance at rent parties and wrote eight ragtime songs, all of which he called "Charleston." The dance later appeared on Broadway in 1923 in *Runnin' Wild.* The "Charleston" went on to become the signature dance of the Roaring Twenties.

In time, South Carolina musicians began to leave the state and became celebrities in their own right. Many were trained at Jenkins Orphanage. William "Cat" Anderson became the lead trumpet player with Duke Ellington's big band and is recognized as one of the greatest high-note trumpet players of all time. He was put in the orphanage after his parents died and took on the name "Cat" for his fighting style.

Other well-known trumpeters were Gus Aiken, Herbert Lee "Peanuts" Holland and Cladys "Jabbo" Smith. Freddie Green, noted for his sophisticated

Dancing the Charleston to the music of the Jenkins Orphanage band. *Courtesy Charleston Museum, Charleston, South Carolina.*

rhythm guitar, played for the Count Basie orchestra. Rufus Jones played in the Duke Ellington orchestra and other bands. Edmund Thornton Jenkins studied at the Avery Institute and traveled to England with the Jenkins Orphanage band. He later played in England and Paris. Lonnie Hamilton III is still influencing Charleston jazz. Students who sing his praises include Charleston's own percussionists Quentin Baxter and Alphonse Mouzon, two talented artists in their own right.

During the 1980s, Spoleto Festival USA in Charleston, Columbia's Main Street Jazz and the Hilton Head Jazz Society started bringing celebrity musicians to South Carolina. Educational institutions added jazz to their curricula. The South Carolina Jazz Hall of Fame was founded at South Carolina State College to honor outstanding students, professionals and support personnel; Dizzy Gillespie, a native of Cheraw, South Carolina, was its first professional inductee. Jazz performances have since become part of the regular programming on local educational television and radio broadcasts.

There is an effort underway to ensure that the Lowcountry's jazz heritage is preserved and promoted. In 2003, Jack McCray and Dr. Karen Chandler authored *Charleston: A Cradle of Jazz* and cofounded the Charleston Jazz Initiative, a project that explores the Lowcountry African American jazz legacy starting in the late nineteenth century. The Jazz Initiative has collected oral histories and gathered a wealth of written information, musical scores, recordings, videos, film clips and photographs about jazz musicians who were natives of or were trained in Charleston. The materials are housed in the Avery Research Center for African American History and Culture at the College of Charleston.

Another American musical genre is gospel. White gospel started with the nineteenth-century Evangelical movements that spread across the country, and black gospel began in the early twentieth century when African Americans migrated to urban centers. This next evolutionary step in black music began along the South Carolina coast and included chants, shouts, field hollers, blues, rags and jazz. Many worship services were held in private homes. To accommodate more people, according to local Gullah historian Alphonso Brown, the people in the black communities built single-room "prays" houses for their worship services. A "prays" (not "praise") house is preserved today at McLeod Plantation on James Island.

Drummer Quentin Baxter has his roots in the African American worship trdition. While in his teens, Quentin Baxter was regarded as one of the most "in demand" musicians in gospel and was first call for numerous regional concerts. He went on to receive a degree in music theory and composition from the College of Charleston. In 1993, he started playing with Oscar Rivers, a local jazz musician who became his mentor and taught Quentin how to listen to the LPs of the great jazz musicians like Miles Davis, Dizzy Gillespie and Monty Alexander. He quickly made the transition from church music to jazz. Since that time, he has had the opportunity to play in regional, national and international performances. In 2003, he teamed up with Jack McCray, author and writer for the *Post and Courier*, and formed the Franklin Street Five, which performed live jazz at the housing project surrounding the old Marine Hospital, now a public building that is lasting monument to the Jenkins Orphanage legacy.[111]

In the 1930s, the Jenkins Orphanage was relocated to a fifty-acre farm on a bluff overlooking the Ashley River. It later changed its name to the Jenkins Institute for Children and today houses only a handful of young girls who are in protective custody. Without the support of a traveling band or a farm, the trustees are hoping to sustain the Jenkins Institute by developing its valuable riverfront property just off Azalea Drive in North Charleston.[112]

Marshlands

Charlestonians were delighted when the U.S. Navy announced in 1960 that it planned to expand the Naval Shipyard to accommodate larger ships and Polaris submarines. There was just one little problem: on the site selected for a $15.6 million dry dock stood Marshlands, an unoccupied plantation house that had to be removed. Saving it would prove to be as monumental a feat as getting the Congressional appropriations in the first place.

Marshlands was a ghostly reminder of the lifestyle of the Lowcountry rice planter aristocracy. As early as 1680, rice had been successfully grown in South Carolina. By the early eighteenth century, Carolina Gold, as the rice was known, had become a commercial staple that, in time, would bring princely fortunes to those who produced it. The rice industry was located in the low-lying coastal areas where the crops could be irrigated by the ebb and flow of the tides.

The great Carolina plantations were managed on the English model; there were three high positions: butler, coachman and patroon. The butler was chief of servants and ensured a rigid adherence to protocol and etiquette. The coachman was charged with maintaining the stable and took pride in teaching the children horsemanship; it was he who proudly drove the family coach and four and administered plantation life for his master, meting out discipline as required. The patroon had charge of the boats, trained the hands to row and taught them plaintive, humorous chants as they bent to the stroke. Of necessity plantations had to be self-sufficient, so there were also carpenters, blacksmiths, coopers, tailors and shoemakers, as well as a hospital for the sick and a house for the children when the mothers were at work. In short, early plantations were communities unto themselves.[113]

The Ball family was part of the elite Lowcountry planter oligarchy. Collectively, they owned large tracts of land in the parishes of St. James Santee, St. Johns Berkeley and St. Stephen in the vicinity of Hell Hole and Wambaw Swamps.

In 1810, during the height of the expanding rice industry, John Ball Jr. built an elegant house on the Cooper River. Called Marshlands, the cypress house was built on an arched brick foundation with a wide single porch and an interior adorned with handsome Adam ornamentation and lavish gouge work. (A similar house, also called Marshlands, was built by James Robert Verdier in Beaufort several years later.)

John Ball Jr., youngest child of John Ball and Lydia Child Chicken Ball, was born at Pompion Hill (later known as Longwood) in 1782. He was descended from Affra Harleston's nephew by marriage and heir, Elias Ball. Educated at Harvard, young John considered entering the ministry but was said to have been dissuaded by his uncle Elias Ball, who told him, "Marry Betsy Bryan, and I will settle you at Comingtee." He duly married his cousin, Elizabeth Bryan, in 1804 and was settled at Comingtee. The couple had five children before Elizabeth died in 1812 about a fortnight after baby John's birth. Ball later married the widow of Thomas Simons and had three more children. He died in 1834 of "country fever" (malaria) contracted at Comingtee.[114]

Elias Ball. (The red cap in the portrait was reportedly worn to conceal baldness.) *Courtesy Margaret Simons Middleton family.*

Ball sold Marshlands to Nathaniel Heyward in 1819. Heyward was one of the leading rice producers, with production in 1815 reported to be in excess of four thousand tons. At the time of his death in 1851, Heyward's estate was the largest in South Carolina. With fifteen plantations and 1,648 slaves, it was assessed at more than $3 million.[115] Acclaimed by his peers as the most successful rice planter of his time, Heyward, in his will, divided his vast holdings among his nine children.[116] Marshlands was passed on to Heyward's daughter and was acquired by Wallace Lawton in 1880. The final change of title occurred with the navy purchase in 1901.

In 1889, the secretary of the navy had estimated that the United States ranked twelfth among the world's naval powers, somewhere below Turkey and China. Before 1900, most steel ships were produced at civilian shipyards, and many of the navy's ships were still wooden. The beginning of expanded military involvement overseas occurred after the Spanish-American War, when the United States acquired its far-flung territories. By 1907, as a result of Progressive Era expansion, President Teddy Roosevelt could dispatch the "Great White Fleet" (battleships were painted white) to trouble spots around the world. By 1910, the United States Navy was the world's third-ranking naval force, second only to those of Great Britain and Germany. After the opening of the Panama Canal, by 1914, the United States could rapidly deploy its military almost anywhere.

To achieve this ascendancy, the government developed shore-based operations, including creation of the Charleston Naval Shipyard. In turn-of-the-century South Carolina, a new dry dock at Port Royal already existed. But it was too small to handle then-modern ships, and worse, it was infested with shipworms. Strong lobbying led by Benjamin R. "Pitchfork Ben" Tillman, a member of the Senate Naval Affairs Committee, and Charleston mayor J. Adger Smyth helped persuade the navy to build on the Cooper River instead of expanding the Port Royal facility.

In 1901, the navy acquired 258 acres of Marshlands plantation, including the house, plus an additional 171 acres in Chicora Park, an unfinished city park just north of Charleston. The navy proceeded to build dry docks, piers, quays and bulkheads on the waterfront, as well as structures related to ship construction and repair nearby. Administrative and storage buildings were located in the interior portion of the yard. The Marshlands mansion was originally used as quarters for the captain of the Naval Shipyard and later housed the production officer until nearby expansion rendered the house unsuitable for domestic habitation.[117]

Since the mansion was located near the repair piers and dry docks, its site had long been desired for expanded production. In 1940, demolition had been narrowly averted by the vigorous opposition of Charleston preservationists. The house was threatened once again in 1960 when its riverfront site was selected for the new dry dock facilities.

Rear Admiral K.M. McManus, commandant of the Sixth Naval District, met with John Muller and several other members of the Society for the

The U.S. Atlantic Fleet, Charleston, South Carolina, circa 1912. *Courtesy Library of Congress.*

Preservation of Old Dwellings (Preservation Society) to inform them that the navy did not have $100,000 to relocate and restore the building at the naval base. The admiral gave them a tour of the uninhabited house and suggested that the society might like to remove the architectural elements before it was razed.

The laws regulating the disposal of government property required that the Marshlands house be: a) donated to a public body if it were too costly to maintain; b) put up for sale through competitive bidding; or c) demolished. The navy offered to give Marshlands to any legal public body that would pay for its removal. Charleston's preservation community asked the City of Charleston to finance moving the house, but officials said that they could not spend $10,000 of public funds to do so. People started scurrying around trying to find a way to save Marshlands.[118]

The preservation community was somewhat relieved when members of Stone Mountain Memorial indicated that they wanted to acquire the house for their Confederate Museum outside of Atlanta. Imagine their horror when they were informed the following week that the memorial committee merely intended to ship architectural elements from the mansion piecemeal to Georgia along with the bricks from the demolished Calvary Chapel on Beaufain Street and artifacts from the dismantled 145-year-old Riley House.

The Preservation Society managed to locate a suitable site on James Island that was owned by the College of Charleston. Unfortunately, the college lacked funds to finance the move. In mid-August 1961, the admiral finally

issued an ultimatum: if the Charleston community could not commit to move the house intact by August 28, it was going to the Stone Mountain project.[119]

In 1961, L. Mendel Rivers had represented the First District of South Carolina for twenty years, and he had recently become the ranking member of the House Armed Services Committee. The new position had given Rivers great influence in Congress and in Charleston. *Anything* that concerned the military crossed his desk. If you wanted something done, Mendel Rivers was the man to know.

Since Congressman Rivers had gotten funding for the dock appropriated, ultimately, the Preservation Society turned to him for help. Through a lot of political maneuvering, the City of Charleston arranged for the College of Charleston to move the house at the college's expense to Fort Johnson on James Island. It was an impressive accomplishment wherein Rivers, Mayor Palmer Gaillard, College of Charleston president George Grice and Admiral McManus all joined forces to save the historic house. (To help cover the cost of the move, the Richardson Foundation of New York donated $10,000, and Historic Charleston Foundation donated $2,000.)

Local newspapers carried articles about how the chimneys were removed before the house was put on trucks that transported it to awaiting barges; it was then floated seven miles down the Cooper River to James Island. Due to the expertise of the L.A. Chitwood Housemoving Company, not a single window pane was broken.[120]

Once restored, the College of Charleston's President Ted Stern offered the house as a residence to Duke's dean of students, C. Hilburn Womble,

Marshlands en route to James Island. *Courtesy* Charleston Mercury, *Charleston, South Carolina.*

to entice him leave his tenured position and become part of the College of Charleston team.[121] Marshlands later became part of the South Carolina Marine Resources Center, a partnership that includes NOAA's National Ocean Service, the National Institute of Standards and Technology, the South Carolina Department of Natural Resources, the College of Charleston and the Medical University of South Carolina.

One of Marshlands' chimneys was never properly supported when the house was placed on pilings at its new home; without that stability, cracks in the walls eventually appeared. The legislature appropriated $500,000 to renovate the mansion just before the state's budget meltdown. Because of the meticulous restoration, in 2010 Marshlands received the Preservation Society's prestigious Carolopolis award.[122]

SAVING THE COLLEGE OF CHARLESTON

The College of Charleston was founded in 1770. Among its distinguished founders were Edward Rutledge, Arthur Middleton and Thomas Heyward Jr., signers of the Declaration of Independence, and John Rutledge, Charles Pinckney and Charles Cotesworth Pinckney, signers of the Constitution. Its first president was Reverend Robert Smith, later the first Episcopal bishop of South Carolina. In 1837, the City of Charleston took over control of the school, and it became the nation's first municipal college. To avoid integration, the college again became a private institution in the 1950s and selected a distinguished scholar, Walter Raleigh Coppage, to be its president. Without city funding, however, the college incurred a substantial deficit, and Dr. Coppage was asked to resign. This was the state of affairs when Captain Theodore S. Stern arrived at the College of Charleston in 1968.

Stern had an impressive array of credentials. His family were well-connected businessmen in New York City. His godfather and mentor was Robert Moses, the man of vision who is credited with building more public works than anyone in the world since the pyramids. Stern followed in the family footsteps and had a distinguished career in the United States Navy long before he was tapped to be president of the College.

In high school, young Stern had excelled in swimming and had won the New York City private school oratorical contest sponsored by the *New York Times*. At Johns Hopkins, he served as a class officer every year he was there in addition to being an alternate swimmer on the United States Olympic team and involvement in extracurricular activities. As president

Charleston College, 1909, Haines Photograph Company. *Courtesy Library of Congress.*

of the Student Activities Council, he was the lone student representative on the board of trustees that recommended that Johns Hopkins University continue providing "undergraduate" education and not be limited to graduate studies only.[123]

Stern enlisted in the Baltimore Navy Reserve on October 16, 1940. Without warning, two days later, President Roosevelt activated a *single* military reserve unit in the United States armed forces: the Baltimore Navy Reserve. Several days later, a surprised Stern found himself a seaman second class aboard the USS *Washington* bound for defense of the Panama Canal. At that time, the navy was ill-prepared to take care of prewar personnel build up. Because of his education and athletic abilities, Stern found himself quickly promoted to ensign; he was charged with establishing athletic and recreational programs. Although reluctant to take the assignment, he succeeded so well that inspectors said it was one of the best operations they had observed. In appreciation, Stern became the personnel officer at the Coco Solo Naval Air Station in Panama. After Pearl Harbor he was promoted to lieutenant (junior grade), responsible for establishing a seaplane base on an isolated beachhead in Ecuador, where he was later decorated for helping earthquake victims. Success led to another promotion. Stern was tasked with planning for advance naval bases in the Pacific theater; he was privileged to work with General Douglas MacArthur and Admirals William F. Halsey and Chester Nimitz throughout the remainder of the war—on projects including plans for the invasion of Japan.[124]

The navy wanted Stern to stay in after the war. There was a problem, however, he was too old to enter the regular navy as a line officer. The only career path was the Navy Supply Corps. Stern accepted the new challenge and attended the Supply Corps School, where he received the first military training of his career. At age thirty-five, he was "Poppa" to classmates fresh out of the Naval Academy. Upon graduation, he received a plum assignment: senior supply officer of the USS *St. Paul CA73*, then flagship of the Pacific Fleet. After the supply officer for the West Pacific Fleet was reassigned, that additional responsibility was added to Stern's original job.

In 1949, Stern was put in charge of the largest navy fuel depot in the United States, located in the area of Norfolk, Virginia; there he learned to become an expert on oil. By the time the Suez Canal crisis erupted in 1956, Stern was at the Pentagon working for the chief of naval operations, Admiral Arleigh Burke. Suddenly, he found himself preparing daily intelligence reports for President Eisenhower that detailed the location of every tanker in the world, the world situation and the military oil resources. Dubbed the "Oil King," Stern appeared before Senator Hart's committee, where he once commented that "Napoleon said an army runs on its stomach, but modern armed forces run on *oil*." Stern also testified before Charleston's Congressman L. Mendel Rivers, the chairman of the House Armed Services Committee. Although Rivers had a reputation for a biting tongue when people tried to skirt issues, he liked reports from the competent naval officer—something that proved to be an asset later on.

In 1958, Stern was assigned to the Armed Forces Industrial College in Washington, D.C., and later became responsible for developing data-processing systems for navy supply centers, depots and storage facilities. Not surprisingly, in 1965 he was tasked with developing a Naval Supply Center in Charleston. The new facility was a state-of-the-art mechanized storage system that tracked over one million spare parts for Polaris submarines and Vietnam War escalation. The supply center also provided food for more than 100,000 personnel—some 60,000 of whom were home ported at the navy base or serving at the air force base.

In spite of his talents, Captain Stern's age was working against him; he was too old to be promoted to admiral. With retirement looming, Comptroller General Elmer Staats inquired if Stern would consider becoming his deputy in the General Accounting Office, and the CEO of AVCO approached him about becoming an executive vice-president. Stern's future seemed bright indeed.

Noting Stern's reputation for being able to get things done, Bevo Howard,[125] Sonny Hanckel and other College of Charleston alumni put out feelers about his accepting the presidency. Stern had been to the college campus only once—at the behest of his wife, who had been asked to represent Hood College at Dr. Walter Coppage's inauguration. Stern was not particularly interested in their overtures.

Finally, House Armed Services Committee chairman Mendel Rivers, then at the height of his political influence, approached him. "We need a president of *my* college." Stern mentioned the prestigious job offers, to which Rivers half-jokingly replied, "I appreciate that, but don't forget that the deputy comptroller general must be approved by Congress, and I know the CEO of AVCO."

Feeling a bit outmaneuvered, Stern inferred he should accept the offer and countered that it would take ninety days to get out of the navy. Rivers replied, "Take the position, and I'll get you out in two weeks." Rivers kept his word, and on August 31, he was the guest speaker at Stern's retirement ceremonies.[126] Rivers later inserted his comments in the *Congressional Record*, praising Captain Stern as a "truly great American."[127]

When he was recruited, Stern had been told that the college was in bad financial shape, but he didn't realize just how bad until he arrived on the scene. There were no financial controls, and the college had a $200,000 deficit. Enrollment was 432 students. Stern's annual salary was the princely sum of $12,000, and he was unable to occupy the president's house because the college had rented it to Avram and Marlene Kronsberg. Stern immediately cut costs by omitting the customary inauguration festivities.

One of the first acts of the new president was to obtain a $300,000 grant from Charleston County Council. This helped rescue the school for the short term.

The year Stern became president, unbeknownst to the public, he was informed of the "accreditation crisis." The Southern Association of Colleges and Schools (SACS) was in the process of taking away the school's accreditation because of deficit spending and library inadequacies—in fact, the papers were already

President Stern presiding at a College of Charleston commencement. *Courtesy College of Charleston Special Collections Library, Charleston, South Carolina.*

being prepared. Fortunately, after liaising with numerous major southern university presidents, Stern was able to persuade SACS to put the college on probation while deficiencies were addressed. Stern committed to build a new library, get an experienced financial officer and employ a distinguished dean of faculty. Quite a tall order for a brand-new college president with no academic experience!

Accreditation standards required 100,000 volumes and library seats for 10 percent of the student body. The library could seat far less, and many books were stored in cartons at 9 Green Street. Perhaps this explained why many students were not serious about their studies. (Marlene Kronsberg later married Nathan Addlestone; they donated funds for the current College of Charleston library.)

Meanwhile, the South Carolina legislature had determined that the Lowcountry needed a comprehensive state institution of higher learning. The question was whether it would create a new university or select an existing facility. The College of Charleston Board of Trustees was faced with the dilemma of competing with another local institution or offering the school to the state. The trustees finally agreed on the latter; then they had to get the blessing of the legislature.

At that time, political strongmen ruled everything in South Carolina, and the strongmen were the "Barnwell Ring." The Speaker of the House was Sol Blatt, and the president pro tem of the Senate was Edgar Brown, both from Barnwell. The only way to get legislative support was with their approval. But Blatt was a University of South Carolina sports fan and Brown was a Clemson man; neither wanted any institution competing with their alma mater.

Stern needed some political clout, so he contacted Joe Riley Sr., who enlisted the help of Mendel Rivers, and the three agreed to go to Barnwell to get Speaker Blatt's support. Somebody suggested that they take along a bottle of "Old Crow" whiskey. The group arrived in a private plane provided by Bill France, the originator of NASCAR, something not lost on Blatt when he met them at the airport with his Lincoln limousine. They drove to Blatt's office, which was conspicuously adorned with Carolina sports paraphernalia. Blatt was vehemently opposed to any funding that threatened his university and said so. Finally, upon a wink from Rivers, Stern picked up the bag with the "Old Crow" and suggested they go over to Blatt's for a friendly drink. Blatt invited them to stay for dinner, and by the time they finished the bottle, Sol Blatt was Ted Stern's close friend. Blatt even offered him a desk in the Speaker's office whenever Stern was lobbying in Columbia.

Now Mendel Rivers had once served in the state legislature, and he knew how things worked in Columbia. The bill to establish the College of Charleston and Francis Marion College came up in July 1970. Rivers felt that the bill had a better chance of passing if he were present. When the vote was taken, Chairman Rivers sat very conspicuously next to Speaker Blatt. Rumors still persist that Rivers's staffer, Mendel Davis, stood nearby, notebook in hand, just in case he had to jot down the names of naysayers. The measure passed unanimously.

That left turning Senator Brown, who was as adamant for Clemson as Blatt had been for South Carolina. It took courting to convince the senator that he would not harm Clemson or help South Carolina if the College of Charleston became part of the state-supported university system. In the end, the bill also passed in the Senate.[128]

To get a distinguished faculty dean, Stern pulled another rabbit out of the hat. He selected C. Hilburn Womble, a Johns Hopkins PhD, who was then dean of students and professor of classics at Duke University. Stern invited him to Charleston, and they got along famously. To entice him, Stern offered Womble the restored 1812 Marshlands mansion at Fort Johnson for his residence. Womble accepted the position and became Stern's right-hand man; he remained at the college until he was tapped as president of Coker College in Hartsville, South Carolina.

Another challenge was expanding the campus. At the suggestion of Bob Figg, an alumnus who was dean of the South Carolina Law School, they set up the College of Charleston Foundation to prevent nearby property owners from excessively jacking up the prices as the college

Speaker Sol Blatt and President Stern. *Courtesy College of Charleston Special Collections Library, Charleston, South Carolina.*

acquired land. Properties were appraised by Elliot Hutson and Joe Riley Sr. before the foundation purchased them at no more than 10 percent over the appraised value. The college acquired about eighty parcels, and only once was the threat of condemnation used. In addition, the foundation prevented gifts to the college from becoming part of the state's general operating fund, and it also enabled the college to issue construction revenue bonds.[129]

With the legal mechanism in place, plans for the new campus commenced. Stern felt strongly that the college should remain where it had started, in downtown Charleston. To embrace the community, he met with local civic leaders, the chamber of commerce and the Rotary Club. He worked with preservationists, especially Francis Edmunds (president of the Historic Charleston Foundation), Tom Stevenson, Peter Manigault and Liz Young and Jane Thornhill at the Preservation Society. Once consensus was reached, the firm of Geiger McIlvain and Kennedy from Columbia was hired to create a master plan.

The campus was basically a square block bounded by Green Street on the north, George to the south, St. Philip to the east and Coming and College Streets to the west. Because of traffic considerations, College and Green Streets were closed. Stern petitioned to close George Street as well, but this failed because of resistance by several prominent donors and the now defunct Kerrisons Department Store, which claimed that traffic modifications would destroy its waning business. Anticipated growth was to expand to a slightly larger block extending from Calhoun to Wentworth Streets, with Coming and St. Philip Streets designated as the outside perimeter.

Historic Randolph Hall became the campus epicenter. Albert Simons, Charleston's great twentieth-century classical architect, designed its remodeling. Stern established a policy that no buildings would be taller than Randolph Hall. When they restored the iconic building, they found bricks laid in the herringbone pattern in the basement. The bricks had originally been ballast on sailing ships. Stern hated patched asphalt pavements and suggested herringbone brick walkways—a seemingly small detail that has unified the diverse campus architecture.[130]

During the accreditation crisis, Stern had promised SACS that a library would be built immediately. O. Johnson Small, a member of the board of trustees, was influential in getting substantial contributions from his brother Robert, a 1936 alumnus who was the chairman and CEO of Dan River Mills. This generosity enabled the college to get the authority to issue revenue bonds; loan repayment was pledged through student library fees. The library was appropriately named after its benefactor, Robert Small.

For more than a century, four years of Latin or Greek had been the graduation requirement for a degree of Bachelor of Arts, making the college the United States' only institution whose BA graduates could transfer to Oxford University without taking an entrance examination. (A student who did not take four years of both Latin and Greek received a Bachelor of Science degree even if he/she had taken no science courses and had majored in English or French literature.) But by 1970, there was a great demand for business education and other, more modern disciplines. So the curriculum was expanded, and more relevant departments were added.

Stern knew most students by name, expected good performance and usually got it. Through good recruiting, college enrollment had grown in ten years from 432 to more than 5,000. Eddie Ganaway, the first black student, entered without incident.

When antiwar activism was in full swing, the national news was full of stories about incidents perpetrated by unruly college students. But not in Charleston! Frank Hunt, a Channel 4 reporter, went to the student union to enquire why there was no protesting. "That guy [Stern] would kill us," they replied. Not satisfied, Hunt went to Stern's home and asked his wife, Alva, the same question. She replied, "His children feel the same way."

President Stern chats with students. *Courtesy College of Charleston Special Collections Library, Charleston, South Carolina.*

Another jewel in Stern's crown was the acquisition of Dixie Plantation, home of naturalist and artist John Henry Dick. The two men met through a mutual friend, Ferdie Waring, and became fast friends. They discussed what should be done with the 862-acre Stono River property after Dick's death; Stern was instrumental in its being given to the college. After the Department of Marine Biology was created, Dick invited graduate students to study the plantation's unique pond ecosystems (one fresh water, one brackish and one salt water). Dick also bequeathed the college his personal artworks and a priceless collection of rare bird books, including original folios of Audubon engravings. Plans are now underway to expand Dixie into an elaborate facility, complete with housing, field stations and a visitor center.

Stern was an extremely popular president. In appreciation for his leadership, the trustees decided to name the student center in his honor; the faculty independently did the same thing. Not knowing of these decisions,

The 1975 groundbreaking of the College of Charleston Student Center. *Left to right*: daughter Elizabeth, President Stern, daughter Carol and Alva Stern. *Courtesy College of Charleston Special Collections Library, Charleston, South Carolina.*

the Student Government Association also made that same recommendation. The Stern Student Center was dedicated in 1975.

Stern's college mentor had told him, "It's better to retire too early than five seconds too late." After ten years at the helm, Stern heeded that advice and submitted his resignation. He went on to guide the nascent Spoleto festival into the monumental success that it is today.

In 1995, in recognition of his community leadership, Stern was named one of ten Charlestonians who shaped the twentieth century by a distinguished committee composed of Walter Edgar, Harlan Greene, Cynthia Jenkins, Robert Rosen and Gene Waddell.

In retirement, Stern still goes to an office at the alumni house dedicated to his use. Hanging behind his desk is a poster of Robert Moses's 100th birthday commemoration. Throughout his life, Stern has tried to embody the civic-minded standards set by his godfather. In doing so, he has discovered that life's greatest joys are in giving.

DYNAMIC DUO
BRAVES THE BULLDOZER

E njoying state support, in 1970 the College of Charleston campus was in full expansion. To make way for the new library, two buildings on Green Street were scheduled to be torn down one Friday morning. The planners, however, had not taken into consideration two feisty, determined Charleston matrons.

Jane Lucas Thornhill and Liz Jenkins Young represent Charleston's second-generation preservationists. They grew up in the Depression, came from well-established families and lived two blocks from each other in downtown Charleston. Both attended St. Michael's Church and were raised in a tradition of great respect for their forebears' accomplishments. After Charleston lost the iconic orphanage on Calhoun Street and the irreplaceable Charleston Hotel on Meeting Street, it was only natural that they were concerned whenever historic buildings were slated for demolition.

The day before the destruction was to take place, Robert Stockton—a reporter for the *News and Courier* who covered education, historic preservation and architecture—had contacted both ladies to get their input on a story he was writing about 8 and 10 Green Street, which were scheduled to be razed. They were historically important because they had been built by Governor William Aiken as rental properties, and the city had already demolished five of Governor Aiken's tenements on Wragg Square to make way for Courtney Elementary School.

Horrified to learn of the impending demolition, the ladies decided that they had to take matters into their own hands. Early the following day, they rushed uptown to Green Street. Pretty, svelte Liz Young knew the driver, Bunt Fiske,

Orphan House (1792), 172 Calhoun Street, Thomas Bennett, architect; cupola (1853–55), Jones and Lee, architectural firm. *Courtesy Charleston Museum, Charleston, South Carolina.*

"Seven Wages," Aiken's Row on Wragg Square. *Courtesy Charleston Museum, Charleston, South Carolina.*

Dynamic Duo Braves the Bulldozer

Charleston Hotel (1839–1960), Charles F. Reichardt, architect. *Courtesy Charleston Museum, Charleston, South Carolina.*

so she did not fear stepping in front of the bulldozer to stop the oncoming behemoth, while her ally, Jane Thornhill, dashed to President Stern's office. Naturally, the bulldozer driver was reluctant to proceed when Mrs. Young told him that she would actually lie down in front of the bulldozer's path if he didn't halt. Jane Thornhill did not fare so well, for President Stern was in New Orleans at a Southern Association of Colleges conference. However, demolition was stopped for the day, and President Stern put an end to it when he returned to Charleston. As a result of the ladies' heroic actions, 10 Green Street remains to this day, and the college created a President's Advisory Council on Historic Preservation. Number 8 Green Street was later demolished.[131]

What would induce seemingly normal, privileged women in a conservative southern town to confront a bulldozer? Charleston women have long enjoyed a reputation for being determined, and these two were no exception.

Elizabeth Jenkins Young grew up on remote Edisto Island in the early twentieth century when it was still an isolated farming community completely separated from the South Carolina mainland. The only access was by boat.

American Indians had lived on Edisto Island for more than three thousand years before the English colonists arrived. Using slave labor, settlers cleared the land and grew cash crops of rice and indigo. After the Revolution, planters turned to long staple cotton, a crop that brought great wealth to the islands off the South Carolina coast; Edisto was reputed to have been the richest of them all.

The Jenkins family was among the early Edisto settlers. In 1669, John Jenkins was mentioned in *The Shaftesbury Papers*, and by the early eighteenth century, John Jenkins Jr. served in the Royal Assembly and owned land on the Edisto River. In 1798, Colonel John Jenkins bought Brick House from Paul Hamilton. This 1725 mansion rivaled the most elegant country estates in the colony. No detail was neglected. The wood was aged for seven years before construction began. Instead of using the more porous local bricks, Hamilton imported dense, harder bricks from Boston. The handsome exterior boasted elaborate stone trim around the windows and entrance, as well as stone quoins at the corners. The interior had a central stair hall and was similar to other grand houses of the period.[132]

Paul Hamilton House (Brick House). *Courtesy College of Charleston Special Collections Library, Waddell Collection, Charleston, South Carolina.*

Dynamic Duo Braves the Bulldozer

The Jenkins family farmed the plantation for the next sixty years. Then secession reared its ugly head. The fervor to secede from the Union was so intense on Edisto Island that their delegate to the Secession Convention, Colonel Joseph Evans Jenkins, passionately thrust the tip of his sword into the table and, as the hilt wavered back and forth, declared, "Gentlemen, if South Carolina does not secede from the Union, Edisto Island will."[133]

Ironically, Edisto Island was the first place in South Carolina declared indefensible after Union troops captured Port Royal, forcing the planter families to evacuate. Colonel Jenkins's son, Edward John Jenkins, was born in 1861 after the family fled to Aiken. The families who returned to Edisto Island after the war found a very different world. Not only was the economy totally devastated, South Carolina was an occupied, defeated Confederate state with a new social order. Life was harsh, and people talked about those painful times well into the twentieth century.

In 1910, widower Edward John Jenkins married Erline Marie Schmetzer from Charleston. She was the teacher in Edisto's one-room school and met Jenkins through his children. There were three children from that marriage.

Living on an island had forced the inhabitants to learn respect for the waters that surrounded it. Young Micah Jenkins knew the river well. He used the tides to commute back and forth as he rowed more than a mile every day to the steamboat landing to collect the mail. The children liked to crab and even taught the family cat how to catch crabs. The most exciting event for the Jenkins children was having picnics on Edisto Beach. They rode horses and read the wonderful book collection in the Brick House library. Fortunately, the boys liked to hunt and fish, for the family depended on their skills to supplement what was grown on the farm.

Mrs. Jenkins was an enterprising woman. She continued to teach in the island's one-room school and ran a summer camp, using the proceeds to send one of her sons to college. She was a great cook. On Thanksgiving, she would set a "big table" for anyone who wanted to join the family. Aside from the pickles and relishes, the menu included wild turkey stuffed with homemade dressing, macaroni and cheese, collards, snap beans and sweet potato pie.

Father Jenkins grew beans and cucumbers. People would come for miles around to buy them. When the automobile came out, Jenkins bought a horseless carriage. Although his sons were "wild to drive it," he wisely did not let them try until it was out of gas. The father's understanding of the automobile, however, was little better than his sons. The boys loved to play tricks on him. Once they put watermelon rinds under the rear wheels

Paul Hamilton House interior after the fire of 1929, Frances Benjamin Johnson, photographer. *Courtesy Library of Congress.*

and laughed uproariously as he pressed the accelerator and the wheels spun furiously.

The idyllic country life abruptly ended when the mansion caught fire in 1929. One evening, Mrs. Jenkins was walking toward the house when she noticed a rosy glow in the attic window. She rushed upstairs to investigate. When she opened the attic door, she was almost instantly engulfed in flames.

Dynamic Duo Braves the Bulldozer

Although the family escaped unharmed, fire consumed everything. It was a devastating loss. In addition to having their home gutted, the eight Jenkins siblings were split up and lived with kindhearted neighbors and relatives until a replacement wooden cottage could be built.

Liz Jenkins met Joseph Rutledge Young at the Yacht Club. Although the Youngs wanted a Charleston wedding at St. Michael's Church, the young couple was married in Trinity Church on Edisto. The couple had three children: Joseph Rutledge Jr., Elizabeth Courtney and Nancy Conner.

The new bride was hardly a typical matron. She became involved in Charleston's civic activities and in 1952 became Charleston's first licensed female tour guide. She toured the city in a green convertible that quickly became her trademark. Some of her interesting guests included Lord Spencer (father of Princess Diana), former U.S. chief justice William Rehnquist and comedian Bob Hope and his wife, Delores.

In 1971, Mayor Palmer Gaillard asked her to help train city guides, and she helped write the book that is still in use today. In 2003, the Charleston Tour Association established the Elizabeth Jenkins Young Award to honor her contributions to the local tour guide industry and made her the first recipient.

It was almost predictable that Liz Young would become an ardent preservationist. She became a trustee of the Historic Charleston Foundation and president of the Society for the Preservation of Old Dwellings.[134] And she became fast friends with Jane Thornhill.

Jane Thornhill came from the Georgetown rice culture. She had among her forebears the brilliant millwright Jonathan Lucas, who came over from England after the Revolution and transformed the rice industry in South Carolina. Before his arrival, removing the outer husks from grains of rice was a labor-intensive process that required hand pounding with wooden mortars and pestles or using crude cog mills powered by animals. Lucas designed mills with rolling screens, elevators and packers; it was not long before his automated rice mills began to dot the Lowcountry. By the early nineteenth century, Lucas had built a toll rice mill on the Ashley River that was driven by water power supplied by a pond near Spring Street. Rice mills enabled Charleston to achieve an enormously lucrative industry that continued until thousands of acres of once profitable rice lay dormant after the Civil War.[135]

Jane Thornhill's father, James Doar Lucas, was born in 1890 at his parents' summer home on South Island near Georgetown. He grew up at Hopsewee, birthplace of Thomas Lynch Jr., the second-youngest signer

Hopsewee Plantation. *Courtesy Charleston Museum, Charleston, South Carolina.*

of the Declaration of Independence. The senior Lynch sold Hopsewee to Robert Hume in 1776, and it remained in the Hume family until the death of his son in 1841. When Hopsewee was sold to settle John Hume's estate, it was purchased by Hume's grandson, John Hume Lucas.

The plantation successfully produced rice until the Civil War. What Yankee soldiers did not take from the house, they gave to the slaves. The family lived in Charleston until 1900, when William Lucas, the eldest son of John Hume Lucas, and his wife moved to back to Hopsewee. They remained there until his death in 1914.

In 1935, John Hume Lucas's widow wrote, "Now the old house is closed and has been for twenty-one years. Will it ever be opened again? Not for the Lucas family in whose possession...it has been for nearly two hundred years. It is taken care of and as much as possible, kept in order, but this once quiet place is now on the Georgetown to Charleston highway, which goes right through the property within a short distance of the residence." The house was sold to International Paper Company in 1945 and is now privately owned.[136]

After he married Jane Larsen, James Lucas went into the shipping business with his father-in-law, Christian Jorgen Larsen. He was from Oslo, Norway, and had been knighted by King Haakon with the Order of St. Olaf at the New York World's Fair in 1939. Larsen was also the Norwegian consul in Charleston, a position that has been passed down through the family to the present. James Lucas fought in the Great War and didn't expect to be called up again, but in World War II, he was called back and served in Iraq, getting supplies for the Russians. His wife never moved out of 49 South Battery. After she married, her husband moved into the Larsen household. Back then there were very few apartments and less money, so newlyweds quite often moved in with other generations.

Young Jane Lucas attended Ashley Hall and spent a pleasant, privileged childhood in downtown Charleston. Her earliest memory was peering up at her Larsen grandfather seated at the head of the dining room table, saying, "Not too much sugar. It is bad for you." Jane and her siblings were dressed in fancy clothes and were taken every day to the Battery with their nurse Sarah Grant. Before her grandparents gave their carriage to the museum in 1929, the children rode in style around the Battery on special occasions. The stock market crash was very depressing for the adults, but it didn't seem to bother the youngsters. They had a grand time running around, for all their friends lived close by.

In September 1938, while the family was having breakfast, Charleston experienced a violent tornado that whizzed near the Larsen dining room as it progressed to Broad and Meeting Streets. It blew a hole in the roof of St. Michael's Church before it caused the collapse of the last section of the city market at East Bay, killing thirty-one people. In the Larsen dining room, the family frantically scrambled to get under the dining room table as doors slammed and glass flew round about. The cook was not so fortunate—she was wedged in the pantry. They had to break down the door with an axe and found her on her knees praying. An irreverent Charlestonian later declared that the tornado was an "act of God," because, he said, "God had been trying to get into St. Michael's Church for two hundred years."

People described Charleston as being "locked up" during the war, but young Jane Lucas "had a blast." Servicemen were everywhere, and like everyone else who wanted to help with the war effort, her mother rented out spare bedrooms to young bachelor officers. The teenage girls were picked up at St. Michael's parish house on Friday evenings to entertain servicemen at Stark Hospital at the navy yard. While in college, students rode "victory bikes" to commute from downtown.

Jane Lucas married Van Noy Thornhill in 1947; they had three children, John Gadsden, Jane Lucas and Theodore Wilbur. In time, Liz Young persuaded her friend to become a tour guide. She took the course issued by Charleston's Historical Commission. In those days, the passing grade was a minimum of 90 out of a possible 100. She conducted tours for a company that went out of business in 1985 and then went out on her own, showing

Liz Young (left) and Jane Thornhill. *Courtesy Jane L. Thornhill.*

Charleston to casual tourists and celebrities like Laura Bush and Garry Trudeau, the *Doonesbury* cartoonist. Jane Thornhill went on to become another tour guide celebrity.

Both Liz Young and Jane Thornhill have received the Preservation Society's coveted Susan Pringle Frost Award and the Frances R. Edmunds Historic Preservation Award from the Historic Charleston Foundation. Both have appeared on television and have been featured in numerous publications. They did almost everything together until Liz Young retired from public life. Jane Thornhill has slowed down only to the extent that her daughter now accompanies her on jaunts around town.

On the south wall of St. Michael's Church there is a marble tablet erected to the memory of the church's first assistant minister, the Reverend Thomas John Young, who died in 1852. In her last years at St. Michael's, Liz Young sat in the pew directly beneath the marker. When the church ended the custom of pew rent, she was the last congregant to sign over her family's pew.

NOISETTE ROSE COMES FULL CIRCLE

John Champneys was one of the many colonials who experimented with horticulture. Son of a royal government official from St. Andrew's Parish[137], he was born in 1743. With his privileged background, he was able to become a successful Charles Town factor (merchant who financed planters) and wharfinger (owner or keeper of a wharf for the purpose of receiving or transporting commercial goods for hire). As a commercial agent who brokered exports and managed dock operations, Champneys built up a lucrative business—so much so that he didn't want to give it up during the Revolutionary War.

Champneys paid a heavy price for his loyalty to the Crown. After the war started, he and his family sailed for London in 1777. They lived there until the British recaptured Savannah from the colonial forces in December 1778. As the occupation of Savannah was part of the strategy to bring the South back under royal control, Champneys set sail for Georgia in 1779 with the expectation of getting back to Charles Town. En route, his ship was captured and taken to Bermuda, where his wife died. In 1780, after the British captured Charles Town, he attempted to return home once again. His vessel was captured, and this time he was diverted to Philadelphia, where one of his children died. On the third attempt, he finally reached Charles Town and resumed his business. His stay was short-lived, for the British evacuated the town in 1782, and Champneys was forced to leave again. He ended up in London, where he hoped to receive restitution for losses incurred by his loyalty to the Crown. Champneys was given £5,000 sterling and again returned to Charleston in 1790. By then, those who had suffered during the British occupation branded him as a traitor, and he never regained his prewar prosperity.

Champneys purchased The Garden, a country estate developed by William Williamson near Jacksonsborough; it had one of the most elaborate gardens in the Lowcountry—ten acres of pleasure grounds devoted to every species of flowering species available.

The Garden allowed Champneys to indulge in botanical interests. About 1802, Champneys crossed two locally available roses, the Old Blush China rose and the Old Musk Rose, creating America's first hybrid rose. Known today as Champneys' Pink Cluster, it was the first rose in the western world that was remontant, or ever-blooming. People have speculated as to the origins of the parent stock, but regardless of the source, Champneys presented his creation to his friend and neighbor, Philippe Stanislas Noisette, a botanist who had left his homeland some time during the French Revolution. The Noisette family had been highly respected gardeners who had worked for the French nobility, and Philippe Noisette carried on the family tradition in the New World. He arrived in Charleston via Santo Domingo and soon established a successful nursery on Charleston Neck. In 1808, he became the director of the Botanical Society.

The Medical College (demolished), Frederick Wesner, architect. *Courtesy Charleston Museum, Charleston, South Carolina.*

Early planters did not practice soil replenishment. Once Champneys's soil was depleted through poor cultivation practices, he moved on to new land on the Georgia coast, where he died in 1820. Before leaving, he gave his nursery stock to the newly formed Charleston Botanical Garden, which had been founded by the Medical College to obtain and propagate plants for medicinal purposes.

Noisette refined Champneys's gift further, and in 1814, he sent his Blush Noisette to his brother in France. Through Champneys's horticultural contacts, it was not long before the fragrant ever-blooming rose became quite the rage.

The delicate rose clusters captured the attention of Joseph Redouté, who had once painted the gardens at Le Petite Trianon as Marie Antoinette's official court artist. He documented gardens that became national property during the French Revolution and the Reign of Terror. Later, under the patronage of Empress Josephine, first wife of Napoleon, he painted her vast rose collection at Malmaison, thus preserving a record of all of the known roses. Redouté's nineteenth-century botanical paintings and engravings made the fragrant pastel blooms of the Noisette rose world famous.[138]

Noisette continued to operate his nursery on Charleston Neck until he died in 1835. His herbarium was left to the administrators of the Garden and Royal Museum of Natural History in Paris, his books were willed to an old friend and his papers and indigenous seeds were given to his brothers in France. Noisette was buried in an unmarked grave at St. Mary's Roman Catholic Church in Charleston; his wife and children left South Carolina after his death.

By the twentieth century, the multiflora Noisette had

Rosa noisettiana by Joseph Redouté. *Courtesy Amelia P. Cathcart.*

been replaced by hybrid tea roses, and in time the delicate blooms could be found mainly in books and colorful magazine articles. It took another South Carolinian to bring the hardy Charleston rose back into vogue.

Ruth C. Knopf started collecting as a hobby in the 1970s. She was married to Reverend John Robert Knopf, pastor of a Baptist church near Edgemoor, South Carolina. When their church built a new parsonage, she had the opportunity to landscape the entire property. She decided to use only plants she really loved. On the "to plant" list was a rose with delicate, small pink blooms that she remembered from her childhood. She soon discovered that the rose was not readily available in local nurseries and thus began a quest for beauty prized by another age.

After discovering Gordon Edward's *Wild and Old Garden Roses* in a bookstore clearance sale, she entered the world of vintage roses and began to read everything available. The big break came when she was invited to see the garden of Ruth Westwood, a rose collector who lived in Newberry, some sixty-five miles from Edgemoor. This generous lady shared the secrets of her lifelong passion—collecting cuttings and propagating vintage roses.

From that time on, Ruth Knopf avidly pursued cuttings of old roses anywhere she wandered: churchyards, grave sites, gardens, wherever the elusive blooms happened to grow (in Texas they call snipping cuttings "rose rustling"). It was not long before she had cultivated a huge backyard planting garden. Like many before her, she began sharing vintage rose cuttings with friends. In time, she discovered the origins of some of the plants, and whenever possible, she began document their provenance. That is how she discovered the link between Noisette roses and Charleston's rich history.

Reverend Knopf died right after Hugo hit South Carolina, and his bereaved wife was forced to vacate the parsonage. During that time of personal tragedy, it had been extremely difficult to leave behind the "growing field" where she had lovingly cultivated roses.

The Knopf family had bought a historic summer house on Sullivan's Island. Due to hurricane damage, everything had to be put in storage while the house was repaired. The movers had forgotten to load a garden worktable, and the recent widow went back to her former home to retrieve it. To her dismay, she discovered that all of her wonderful plantings had been bulldozed into a pile right on top of where she had once cultivated her "friends," the rose cuttings. It was a bitter pill.

Once settled in Charleston, Ruth Knopf became the head gardener at Boone Hall. When the Charleston Garden Festival began holding an event at the Gaillard, she sold heritage roses in one of the booths. She met a lot of people and discovered that most of them did not know much about heritage roses. This gave her the opportunity to begin consulting about growing heritage roses in and around Charleston.

Through the Garden Festival, Ruth Knopf met Patti McGee, Jane Waring and Mimi Cathcart. Their common interest in roses led to Charleston's hosting the Ninth International Heritage Rose Conference in 2001. As part of the preparation, five years before the conference, the steering committee established the Hampton Park Noisette Study Garden and planted the Heritage Rose Trail on key public sites throughout the city. The conference theme was a natural: Noisette roses began in Charleston in the early nineteenth century. The conference was a huge success.

In recognition for her work preserving Noisette roses and her horticultural contributions to the Lowcountry, Ruth Knopf became the first recipient of the Charleston Horticultural Society's prestigious 1830 Award. She has received many other honors since that time. In 2011, she was honored for her work popularizing and preserving Noisette and other heritage roses by the famed international organization Great Rosarians of the World. This honor capped decades of propagating roses that originated in Charleston.[139] Collectors continue to appreciate Ruth Knopf's contributions to the wonderful world of roses.

Notes

Introduction

1. "Far from popular misconception, L. Mendel Rivers did not come from poverty. Quite the contrary, his father, Lucius Hampton Rivers, purchased the second brand-new Ford automobile in Berkeley County. At the time of his death in 1914, he was county road commissioner and was in the process of establishing a small political empire outside of St. Stephen, South Carolina. Lucius Hampton Rivers farmed 500 acres of cotton and owned a saw mill, a general store, turpentine still, a cotton gin and extensive timberlands. He stabilized the damage done by the earthquake of 1886 at the nearby St. Stephen Episcopal church. In a cruel reversal of fortune, within seven years of his death, the family lost nearly everything. The eldest son had forged his mother's name to a mortgage in 1920, and when farm prices collapsed in 1921, he was unable to make the payment. When the widow denied having signed the mortgage, she was confronted with the terrible fact that her own son had forged her name. The bank threatened to have her oldest son indicted for fraud and theft unless she consented to having signed the forged document. So she consented, and her eldest son stayed out of prison, disgraced. She lost nearly all of her husband's entire estate, and with what little cash remained, she moved into the remote, unfashionable, industrial district of Charleston County known vaguely as "The North Area," now known as North Charleston. It was a wise move, for she purchased her own home on the relatively fashionable O'Hear Avenue. Large enough to accommodate boarders,

it was situated on the trolley car line just three blocks from the GARCO plant. Far from poverty, L. Mendel Rivers, the son of a country politician-entrepreneur, grew up as a relatively privileged youth in the very small, unsophisticated area where he lived. This dichotomy probably explains the complexity of his nature. Mendel Rivers succeeded because of his larger-than-life personality. He was flamboyant, outrageous, insightful, daring, dramatic, and sometimes even foolhardy. His colleagues on the House Armed Services Committee were impressed and intimidated, and by the sheer force of his personality, he was able to drive his agenda through the committee in spite of the enormous divide in the country during the Vietnam War"—L. Mendel Rivers Jr.

2. Edgar et al., "Magnificent Ten Charlestonians," 32–34.

THE GOOSE CREEK MEN

3. Edgar, *South Carolina*, 36–43.
4. McCrady, *Under the Proprietary Government*, 68–71.
5. Edgar, *South Carolina Encyclopedia*, 346–48, 363.
6. Immigrants from the Caribbean islands include: "Proprietor Sir John Colleton; Governor James Colleton; Major Charles Colleton; Sir John Yeamans, Landgrave and Governor; Captain John Godfrey, Deputy; Christopher Portman, John Maverick, and Thomas Grey, among the first members elect of the Grand Council; Captain Gyles Hall, one of the first settlers and the owner of a lot in Old Town; Robert Daniel, Landgrave and Governor; Arthur and Edward Middleton, Benjamin and Robert Gibbes, Barnard Schinkingh, Charles Buttall, Richard Dearsley, and Alexander Skeene. Among others from Barbados were those of the following names: Cleland, Drayton, Elliot, Fenwicke, Foster, Fox, Gibbon, Hare, Hayden, Lake, Ladson, Moore, Strode, Thompson, Walter, and Woodward. Sayle, the first governor, was from Bermuda. From Jamaica came Amory, Parker, Parris, Pinckney, and Whaley; from Antigua, Lucas, Motte, and Percy; from St. Christopher, Rawlins and Lowndes; from the Leeward Islands: Sir Nathaniel Johnson, the Governor; and from the Bahamas: Nicholas Trott, the Chief Justice," McCrady, *Under the Proprietary Government*, 327–28.
7. Edgar, *South Carolina Encyclopedia*, 384–85. McCrady expands the list to include names from Ms. Poyas's *Olden Time of Carolina*, 36: "Thomas Smith, of Black River, Edward Hyrne; Thomas Smith, son of Landgrave;

Captain George Chicken, Captain Benjamin Schenckingh, Peter St. Julien, Benjamin Godin, Mr. Mazyck, Henroyda Inglish, and Captain John Neve." McCrady further states that Robert Gibbes, Ralph Izard and so on are conspicuously absent from the Poyas list. See *Under the Proprietary Government*, 238.

8. *Collections of the South Carolina Historical Society*, 160.

9. McCrady, *Under the Proprietary Government*, 124.

10. While her husband was at sea, Affra Harleston cleared lands and managed a remote plantation. She inherited her husband's estate in 1695. She died in 1698 and willed her estate to her nephew, John Harleston, and to her husband's half-nephew, Elias Ball. She deeded seventeen acres to the rector of St. Philip's Episcopal Church and his successors. Called the Glebe, it was surrounded by St. Philips, Coming, George and Beaufain Streets. Deas, "Recollections of the Ball Family," 24–25; marker beside the Grace Church parish house, Glebe Street.

11. Edgar, *South Carolina Encyclopedia*, 1,056–57.

12. *Collections of the South Carolina Historical Society*, 169–71.

13. Edgar, *South Carolina*, 85; Middleton, *Affra Harleston*, 18.

14. Edgar, *South Carolina*, 137.

15. "[Southall] had the wisdom to see the usefulness and noble character of the French and Swiss, who were now coming into the province in considerable numbers and filling up waste places in Craven County on the Cooper and Santee, which were soon to blossom under their skilful and laborious cultivation; and the first to constitute them citizens as free born in the colony, and of equal rights with other settlers…under his administration, the first act for the government of negro slaves was passed. This act followed generally the Barbadian slave code; but, in more than one respect, it was an improvement upon that law, especially in providing for the punishment of any one killing a slave. It provided also, for the slaves' comfort, and required that they should have convenient clothes… Southall returned to North Carolina, where he died in 1694; and it is said that much of the wealth he had accumulated there was recovered by those from whom he had unjustly taken it," McCrady, *Under the Proprietary Government*, 233–34.

16. Edgar et al., *Biographical Directory*, vol. 2, 180–82.

17. Ibid., 466–68.

18. Ibid., 335–36.

19. *South Carolina Historical and Genealogical Magazine* 32, 1–2.

20. Eastman and Good, *Hidden History of Old Charleston*, 52–55.

21. Dickerman, *The House of Plant*, 100–1.
22. McCrady, *Under the Proprietary Government*, 489–98; Edgar et al., *Biographical Directory*, vol. 2, 272–73.
23. McCrady, *Under the Proprietary Government*, 468–69.
24. Ibid, 454–55.
25. Ibid, 173.

GENTLEMEN'S PURSUITS

26. McCrady, *Under Royal Government*, 515–24.
27. Irving, *South Carolina Jockey Club*, 34–35.
28. Ibid., 35.
29. Preservation Society of Charleston, "Inside the Gates of Historic Fenwick Hall Plantation," www.fenwickhall.com/fenwickshortstories.html.
30. Ravenel, *Piazza Tales*, 19.
31. McCrady, *Under Royal Government*, 525.
32. Irving, *South Carolina Jockey Club*, 165.
33. Ibid., 203.
34. Ibid., 152.
35. Butler, *Votaries of Apollo*, 68–69.
36. Edgar, *South Carolina Encyclopedia*, 899.
37. Behre, "Charleston Pillars Greet Belmont Fans."
38. Edgar, *South Carolina Encyclopedia*, 350; Baptist History, Lesson 5, 37, www.glorytogloryministries.com.
39. Edgar, *South Carolina Encyclopedia*, 356.
40. Ibid., 727–28.
41. *Constitution of the Bible Society*, 7–19.
42. Nepveux, *George A. Trenholm: Financial Genius*, 98.
43. Gwyn, "Old Book Tells of Bible Distribution Problems"; Lilly, "Charleston Bible Society Has Distinguished History."
44. Eastman, "Charleston Bible Society Celebrates 200 Years."
45. Porter, *Led On!*, 47.

THE DRAYTONS OF DRAYTON HALL

46. Ravenel, *Eliza Pinckney*, 76–77.
47. Ibid., 42–44.

48. Edgar et al., *Biographical Directory*, vol. 2, 201–2.
49. Eastman and Good, *Hidden History of Old Charleston*, 37–38; Steedman, "Charleston's Forgotten Tea-Party."
50. Henning, *Great South Carolinians*, 87.
51. McCrady, *South Carolina in the Revolution*, 74–85.
52. Ibid., 207–9; McCrady, *Under the Proprietary Government*, 495; Edgar, *South Carolina Encyclopedia*, 274–75; Drayton Hall website, www.draytonhall.org.
53. Morgan, *Recollections of a Rebel Reefer*, 262–64.
54. Eastman, "Charles Drayton—Vindicated by Time," parts I and II.
55. In 2004, Cooper Station Holdings of Beaufort bought the 6,600-acre Watson Hill tract from MeadWestvaco and submitted plans for about 4,500 single-family homes and town houses, plus a golf course, recreational facilities, a hotel, churches and commercial buildings directly across from Middleton Place. After developers defaulted on their loan in 2009, MeadWestvaco announced plans to buy back Watson Hill and fold it into its green/conservation-minded development called East Edisto.

Rhett Butler and the Blockade Runners

56. Mitchell, *Gone with the Wind*, 68–69 (introduction), 76–77 (obstacles faced by the Confederacy), 153–62, and 387 (blockade runner), and 429–30 (Confederate treasure).
57. Reverend Dr. A. Toomer Porter was the son of a prosperous and respected planter. He spent three years in business training at the counting house of Robertson & Blacklock, the largest Charleston rice house at that time. After he came of age, he became a planter but felt a calling to enter the ministry. He sold his property and moved back to Charleston, where he started the Church of the Holy Communion. Originally intended for indigent parishioners, it soon attracted wealthy uptown parishioners, including George Trenholm. Porter established the first industrial school for girls in the state. During the war, they made one thousand uniforms for Hampton's Legion. The Freedmen's Bureau stole the sewing machines after the war. In 1866, blind Bishop Davis sent Porter north to raise funds through the Episcopal churches to support a Theological Seminary (something that did not interest northern congregants) and to establish a parochial black school. Trenholm helped with the selection of the condemned Marine Hospital and was one of its six trustees. President Johnson personally contributed $1,000 and expedited passage of the bill

to release the Marine Hospital. The school was the first large black school in the South. Porter was the only surviving trustee when Reverend Jenkins, a black Baptist preacher, obtained a lease for the "Colored Orphanage." The next year, Porter founded a school for impoverished white children and spent the rest of his life raising money to support it.

58. Porter, *Led On!*, 112–13.
59. Nepveux, *George Alfred Trenholm and the Company that Went to War*, 1–6. Edgar, *South Carolina Encyclopedia*, 978.
60. Nepveux, *George A. Trenholm: Financial Genius*, 15–16.
61. Ibid., 24–25.
62. Spence, *Treasures of the Confederate Coast*, 239–40; Nepveux, *George A. Trenholm: Financial Genius*, 106, 151 and 178.
63. Boaz et al., "Dashing Blockade Runner."
64. Nepveux, *George A. Trenholm: Financial Genius*, 58–74.
65. Brown, surgeon of the *Kearsarge*, "*The Duel Between The 'Alabama' And The 'Kearsarge*,'" Home of the Civil War website.
66. Ibid., 140–41.
67. Bivin, *America's Civil War* magazine, May 1995.
68. Hanna, *Flight into Oblivion*, 14–16.
69. Other sources say that William Trenholm accompanied his father to Charleston.
70. Nepveux, *George Alfred Trenholm and the Company that Went to War*, 89–92; Morgan, *Recollections of a Rebel Reefer*, 228–52.
71. Nepveux, *George Alfred Trenholm and the Company that Went to War*, 92.
72. Porter, *Led On!*, 226–30.
73. Nepveux, *George A. Trenholm: Financial Genius*, 181–98.
74. Ibid., 217.
75. Nepveux, *George Alfred Trenholm and the Company that Went to War*, 97–98.
76. Ibid., 224–29.

Tower of the Winds

77. Soros, *James "Athenian" Stuart*, 78.
78. Crook, *Greek Revival*, 7–15, 61.
79. Wiebenson, *Sources of Greek Revival Architecture*, 3–15; Glancy, *Guardian*, March 19, 2007.
80. Crook, *Greek Revival*, 17.
81. Soros, *James "Athenian" Stuart*, 59–89.

82. Waddell, *Charleston Architecture*, 41–43.
83. Courtesy Evan Thompson, director of the Charleston Preservation Society.
84. Other houses with colossal Tower of the Winds columns: Cooper–O'Connor House, circa 1855, 180 Broad Street; Charles Kerrison House, circa 1838, 138 Wentworth Street; and John Hume Lucas (Wycliffe) House, circa 1850–52, 178 Ashley Avenue. Tower of the Winds capitals appear on both on exterior and interior one-story columns throughout the city.
85. Nepveux, *George Alfred Trenholm and the Company that Went to War*, 4–8.
86. Bailey, "Old Flat Rock."
87. *South Carolina Historical and Genealogical Magazine* 65, 98.

CHARLESTON'S RAILROAD TYCOONS

88. West Brookfield Historical Commission, 2007.
89. Jones, *Synoptic History for Laymen*, 188.
90. Ibid., 189.
91. Ibid., 190.
92. Eastman, *Remembering Old Charleston*, 95–100.
93. Williams, *Hampton and His Red Shirts*, 419.
94. The Parsons traced their English lineage back to the Crusades through Coronet Joseph Parsons, who arrived in the colonies in 1635 aboard the ship *Transport*. He settled in Springfield, Massachusetts, and was a founder of Northampton, Massachusetts. His house, the oldest in Northampton, is now a museum. Thomas Parsons of a later generation moved to Maine in the early eighteenth century and founded Parsonfield. Parsons money built the library in Kennebunk, and the family continued to be prominent in that area. Parsons family branches flourished in both Maine and Massachusetts.
95. Derrick, *Centennial History of South Carolina Railroad*, 822.
96. William Aiken House, National Register of Historic Places.
97. *News and Courier*, May 21, 1894.
98. Chamberlain, "Reconstruction in South Carolina," 473–84. Senator Sumner had been vigorous in keeping ex-Confederates from regaining the power they had enjoyed before the war. Sumner was removed from his chairmanship in 1871 after he alienated President Grant. A spurned reformer, he joined the more conciliatory Liberal Republican Party.

99. Porter, *Led On!*, 439–40.
100. Williams, *Hampton and His Red Shirts*, 408.
101. *News and Courier*, May 19, 1894.
102. Derrick, *Centennial History of South Carolina Railroad*, 266–67.
103. Ibid., 280–81.
104. Poston, *Buildings of Charleston*, 95–96.
105. Preservation Society marker, 2007.
106. Parker, "Variety of Architectural Styles."
107. Birmingham, "Fire Damages Oaks Clubhouse."

A MODERN WADE HAMPTON AND HIS LADY

108. Rivers et al., *Mendel and Me*, 199–201.
109. *Time* magazine, "South Carolina: Quarterback Sneak"; Charles D. Ravenel Papers, University of South Carolina Library Gifts.
110. Eastman, "Ann Darlington Edwards," parts I, II and III.

JAZZ AND RAZZMATAZZ

111. Eastman, "Quentin Baxter—Palmetto State's Versatile Jazzman" and "Jack McCray, Author, Journalist, and Jazz Aficionado."
112. See Kropf's article in the August 21, 2010 *Post and Courier*.

MARSHLANDS

113. McCrady, *Under the Proprietary Government*, 515–17.
114. Deas, "Recollections of the Ball Family," 135.
115. National Register of Historic Places, Marshlands Plantation House.
116. Heyward's plantation house on the Combahee River was destroyed by Yankee raiders on June 23, 1863, when Colonel Montgomery's First South Carolina Black Regiment came up from Port Royal by steamer. A description of this raid is in the July 3, 1863 *Charleston Mercury*. The land remained in the Heyward family until it was bought by the Du Ponts in 1911. Pledger, Plantation's "Piles of Trash."
117. National Register of Historic Places, Charleston Navy Yard Historic District.

118. According to family tradition, Arden Ball Howard, wife of Bevo Howard, renovated fourteen buildings, many of which would have otherwise been demolished. She, too, wanted to rescue Marshlands, for it was part of the Ball legacy. She located a lot on the corner of Murray and Lenwood Boulevards, hired an engineer to do a feasibility study and interviewed Mr. Chitwood, the house mover. Her friends and family poked fun at the impossible scheme. The idea was dropped after the engineer said that it was impossible to raise the house over the low battery near the Coast Guard Station.
119. *Charleston Evening Post*, 1961.
120. Rivers et al., *Mendel and Me*, 83–85; Stern, *No Problems, Only Challenges*, 79; *News and Courier*, "Marshlands Fate Once in Question"; *Preservation Progress*, "Marshlands Plantation House at the Navy Yard."
121. Stern, *No Problems, Only Challenges*, 78–79.
122. Behre, "Marshlands Makeover"; Eastman, "Saving Marshlands," *Charleston, Mercury*, April 21, 2011.

SAVING THE COLLEGE OF CHARLESTON

123. Stern, *No Problems, Only Challenges*, 1–33.
124. Ibid., 38–48.
125. Beverly "Bevo" Howard was a precision flyer who wowed more than 30 million spectators with his flawless exhibitions. His contributions to aviation are highlighted at the Smithsonian, where his biplane, transported from Germany on the *Hindenburg* zeppelin, hangs upside down. He is credited with training more than seven thousand allied combat pilots. Following the war, he established Flight Training programs for the Pakistani Air Force in Jacksonville, Florida. Through Hawthorne School of Aeronautics, he trained more than ten thousand military and civilian pilots at Spence Air Base in Moultrie, Georgia (pronounced "mole-tree" there). When Spence was no longer needed as a training facility, Hawthorne was consolidated into a single base in Charleston. People still talk about how Bevo flew under the span of the Cooper River Bridge in a more relaxed aviation era.
126. Stern, *No Problems, Only Challenges*, 49–61.
127. Rivers, Congressional Record.
128. Stern, *No Problems, Only Challenges*, 62–70; Ravenel, *Rivers Delivers*, 127–28.
129. Stern, *No Problems, Only Challenges*, 72–73.
130. Ibid., 84–88.

DYNAMIC DUO BRAVES THE BULLDOZER

131. Poston, *Buildings of Charleston*, 515.
132. National Register of Historic Places, Brick House.
133. Leifermann, "Out-of-the-Way Isle."
134. Eastman, "Elizabeth Jenkins Young."
135. Edgar, *South Carolina Encyclopedia*, 573.
136. National Register of Historic Places, Hopsewee Plantation.

NOISETTE ROSE COMES FULL CIRCLE

137. Edgar et al., *Biographical Directory*, vol. 2, 151.
138. Kean, *Noisette Roses*, 3–17.
139. Eastman, "Ruth C. Knopf—Renowned Rosarian."

BIBLIOGRAPHY

Bailey, Louise. "Old Flat Rock." Village of Flat Rock, North Carolina. http://www.villageofflatrock.org/quiltinfo.htm

Behre, Robert. "Charleston Pillars Greet Belmont Fans." *Charleston Post and Courier*, June 13, 2005.

———. "Marshlands Makeover." *Charleston Post and Courier*, January 25, 2010.

Birmingham, Nita. "Fire Damages Oaks Clubhouse." *Charleston Post and Courier*, February 7, 2008.

Bivin, Ken. *America's Civil War* magazine, May 1995.

Boaz, Thomas M., and Ethel Seabrook Nepveux, "Dashing Blockade Runner: Captain Thomas J. Lockwood." BNET, CBS Interactive Network, n.d.

Brown, John M., Surgeon of the *Kearsarge*. "The Duel Between The 'Alabama' And The 'Kearsarge'" www.civilwarhome.com/duel.htm.

Butler, Nicholas Michael. *Votaries of Apollo: The St. Cecilia Society and the Patronage of Concert Music in Charleston, South Carolina, 1766–1820*. Columbia: University of South Carolina Press, 2007.

Chamberlain, Daniel. "Reconstruction in South Carolina." *Atlantic Monthly* 87, issue 522 (April 1901): 473–84.

Charles D. Ravenel Papers. University of South Carolina Library Gifts, 1973–96.

Collections of the South Carolina Historical Society. Vol. 5. Richmond, VA: book and job printer William Ellis Jones, 1897.

Constitution of the Bible Society of Charleston, S.C. Charleston, SC: Courier Book and Job Presses, n.d.

Crook, J. Mordant. *The Greek Revival.* London: Butler and Tanner Limited, 1972.

Deas, Anne Simons. "Recollections of the Ball Family of South Carolina and the Comingtee Plantation." Copyright Alwyn Ball Jr. N.p., 1909.

Derrick, Samuel Melanchthon. *Centennial History of South Carolina Railroad.* Columbia, SC: State Company, 1930.

Dickerman, G.S. *The House of Plant of Macon Georgia with Genealogies and Historical Notes.* New Haven, CT: Tuttle, Morehouse & Taylor Co., 1900.

Eastman, Margaret Middleton Rivers. "Ann Darlington Edwards—A Portrait in Grace," parts I, II, III. *Charleston Mercury*, November 4 and 18 and December 2, 2010.

———. "Charles Drayton—Vindicated by Time," parts I and II. *Charleston Mercury*, August 26 and September 9, 2010.

———. "Charleston Bible Society Celebrates 200 Years." *Charleston Mercury Home Magazine*, April 22, 2010.

———. "Elizabeth Jenkins Young." *Charleston Mercury*, November 20, 2008.

———. "Jack McCray, Author, Journalist, and Jazz Aficionado." *Charleston Mercury*, June 4, 2009.

———. "Quentin Baxter—Palmetto State's Versatile Jazzman." *Charleston Mercury*, May 21, 2009.

———. *Remembering Old Charleston: A Peek Behind Parlor Doors.* Charleston, SC: The History Press, 2008.

———. "Ruth C. Knopf—Renowned Rosarian." *Charleston Mercury*, March 16, 2011.

———."Saving Marshlands." *Charleston Mercury*, April 21, 2011.

Eastman, Margaret Middleton Rivers, and Edward Fitzsimons Good. *Hidden History of Old Charleston.* Charleston, SC: The History Press, 2010.

Edgar, Walter. *South Carolina: A History.* Columbia: University of South Carolina Press, 1998.

Edgar, Walter, ed. *The South Carolina Encyclopedia.* Columbia: University of South Carolina Press, 2006.

Edgar, Walter, Harlan Greene, Chythia Jenkins, Robert Rosen and Gene Waddell. "The Magnificent Ten Charlestonians Who Shaped the 20th Century." *Charleston©*, Millennium Issue, 1995.

Edgar, Walter, N. Louise Bailey and Inez Watson. *Biographical Directory of the South Carolina House of Representatives.* Vol. 2, *The Commons House of Assembly 1892–1775.* Columbia: University of South Carolina Press, 1977.

Gwyn, Miles B. "Old Book Tells of Bible Distribution Problems." *Charleston News and Courier*, November 13, 1970.

Hanna, A.J. *Flight into Oblivion*. Bloomington: Indiana University Press, 1959, reprint.

Henning, Helen Kohn. *Great South Carolinians*. Chapel Hill: University of North Carolina Press, 1940.

Irving, John Beaufain. *The South Carolina Jockey Club*. Charleston, SC: Russell and Jones, 1857.

Jones, Louis P. *South Carolina: A Synoptic History for Laymen*. Lexington, SC: Sandpaper Store, 1971.

Kean, Virginia, ed. *Noisette Roses: 19th Century Charleston's Gift to the World*. Santa Rosa, CA: Global Interprint, Inc., 2009.

Kropf, Schuyler. *Charleston Post and Courier*, August 21, 2010.

Leifermann, Henry. "An Out-of-the-Way Isle in South Carolina." *New York Times*, April 3, 1994.

Lilly, Edward G. "Charleston Bible Society Has Distinguished History." *Charleston Evening Post*, November 15, 1973.

McCrady, Edward, LLD. *South Carolina in the Revolution 1775–1780*. Norwood, MA: Macmillan Company, Norwood Press, 1902.

———. *Under Royal Government 1719–1776*. Norwood, MA: Macmillan Company, Norwood Press, 1902.

———. *Under the Proprietary Government 1670–1719*. Norwood, MA: Macmillan Company, Norwood Press, 1902.

Middleton, Margaret Simons. *Affra Harleston and Old Charles-Towne in South Carolina*. Columbia, SC: R.L. Bryan Company, 1971.

Mitchell, Margaret. *Gone with the Wind*. New York: MacMillan Company, 1968.

Morgan, James Morris. *Recollections of a Rebel Reefer*. New York: Houghton Mifflin Company, 1917.

Nepveux, Ethel S. *George A. Trenholm: Financial Genius of the Confederacy, His Associates and His Ships that Ran the Blockade*. Anderson, SC: Electric City Printing Company, 1999.

———. *George Alfred Trenholm and the Company that Went to War*. Anderson, SC: Electric Printing Company, 1994.

News and Courier. "Marshlands Fate Once in Question." December 10, 1961.

News and Courier. May 21, 1894.

Parker, Jim. "Variety of Architectural Styles Found in The Oaks." *Charleston Post and Courier*, January 24, 2004.

Pierson, William H., Jr. *American Buildings and Their Architects*. Garden City, NY: Doubleday and Company, Inc., 1970.

Pledger, George. Plantation's "Piles of Trash," Maritime Research Division, South Carolina Institute of Archaeology and Anthropology, University of South Carolina, n.d.

Porter, A. Toomer, DD. *Led On! Step by Step.* New York: Arno Press, 1967.

Poston, Jonathan H. *The Buildings of Charleston: A Guide to the City's Architecture.* Columbia: University of South Carolina Press, 1997.

Poyas, Elizabeth Ann. *The Olden Time of Carolina.* Charleston, SC: Nabu Press, 2010.

Preservation Progress 6, no. 4. "Two Down and One to Stay" (November 1961).

Preservation Progress 6, no. 1. "Marshlands Plantation House at the Navy Yard" (January 1961).

Ravenel, Harriott Horry. *Eliza Pinckney.* New York: Charles Scribner's Sons, 1896.

Ravenel, Marion Rivers. *Rivers Delivers: The Story of L. Mendel Rivers.* Charleston, SC: Wyrick & Company, 1995.

Ravenel, Rose Pringle. *Piazza Tales.* Charleston, SC: private printing, 2007.

Rivers, L. Mendel. Congressional Record—House, October 11, 1968, Captain Theodore Sanders Stern, Supply Corps, U.S. Navy, Retired, 30767-30768.

Rivers, Margaret Middleton, Margaret M.R. Eastman and L Mendel Rivers Jr. *Mendel and Me: Life with Congressman L. Mendel Rivers.* Charleston, SC: The History Press, 2007.

Soros, Susan Weber, ed. *James "Athenian" Stuart: The Rediscovery of Antiquity.* New Haven, CT: Bard Center for Studies in the Decorative Arts, Design and Culture, Yale University Press, 2007.

South Carolina Historical and Genealogical Magazine 65, no. 2 (April 1964): 98.

South Carolina Historical and Genealogical Magazine 32 (January 1931): 1–2.

Spence, E. Lee. *Treasures of the Confederate Coast: The "Real Rhett Butler" and Other Revelations.* Miami, FL: Narwhal Press, Inc., 1995.

Steedman, Marguerite. "Charleston's Forgotten Tea-Party." *Georgia Review* (1967).

Stern, Theodore S. *No Problems, Only Challenges.* Saline, MI: McNaughton and Gunn, 2001.

Time magazine. "South Carolina: Quarterback Sneak." October 14, 1974.

U.S. Department of the Interior, National Park Service. National Register of Historic Places, Brick House, Edisto Island, South Carolina, February 10, 1984.

U.S. Department of the Interior, National Park Service. National Register of Historic Places, Charleston Navy Yard Historic District, February 14, 2006.

U.S. Department of the Interior, National Park Service. National Register of Historic Places, Hopsewee Plantation, June 4, 1971.

U.S. Department of the Interior, National Park Service. National Register of Historic Places, Marshlands Plantation House, March 30, 1973.

U.S. Department of the Interior, National Park Service. National Register of Historic Places, William Aiken House, Associated Railroad Structures, May 12, 1981.

Waddell, Gene. *Charleston Architecture 1670–1860*. Volume II. Charleston, SC: Wyrick and Company, 2003.

Wiebenson, Dora. *Sources of Greek Revival Architecture*. London: A Zwemmer Limited, 1969.

Williams, Alfred B. *Hampton and His Red Shirts: South Carolina's Deliverance in 1876*. Charleston, SC: Walker, Evans and Cogswell Company, 1935.

ABOUT THE AUTHOR

A native Charlestonian, Margaret (Peg) M.R. Eastman was a professional guide at Winterthur Museum in Delaware and has been a consultant on preparing job documentation for regulatory compliance in highly hazardous industries. She coauthored *Process Industry Procedures and Training Manual*, published by McGraw Hill. She coauthored *Mendel and Me: Life with Congressman L. Mendel Rivers* and *Hidden History of Old Charleston* and authored *Remembering Old Charleston*, all published by The History Press. Currently, she is a freelance writer for the *Charleston Mercury* and has lectured on Charleston architecture. She is involved with the Preservation Society's Master Conservation program.

www.ingramcontent.com/pod-product-compliance
Lightning Source LLC
Chambersburg PA
CBHW060804100426
42813CB00004B/936